IT TaKes
a VILLaGeR

Also by Arnold Hano

Fiction
3 Steps to Hell: So I'm a Heel/Flint/The Big Out
The Big Out
The Executive
Marriage Italian Style (movie tie-in)
Bandolero (movie tie-in)
Running Wild (movie tie-in)

Sports
A Day in the Bleachers
Sandy Koufax: Strikeout King
Willie Mays: The Say-Hey Kid
The Greatest Giants of Them All
Roberto Clemente: Batting King
Willie Mays: Mr. Baseball Himself
Kareem! Basketball Great
Muhammad Ali, the Champion

Written as Gil Dodge
Flint

Written as Mathhew Gant
Valley of Angry Men
The Manhunter
The Last Notch
The Raven and the Sword
Queen Street

Written as Ad Gordon
The Flesh Painter
Slade

Written as Mike Heller
So I'm a Heel

To Diane —

IT TaKes
a VILLaGeR

Wit and Wisdom
by Laguna's Irreverent Observer

Arnold Hano

Arnold Hano
5/FU/18

Laurel Press
Laguna Beach, California

ISBN: 978-0-9670376-5-3

Library of Congress Card Number: 2013935736

Printed in the United States of America

For Village Laguna

Table of Contents

Photography Credits

In addition to the photographs credited to the photographers listed below, many thanks go to numerous people who helped search for appropriate photographs for this book. These people include but are not limited to Mark Chamberlain, Ann Christoph, Gene Felder, Jackie Gallagher, Charlotte Masarik, and Jinger Wallace.

Photographers:
Mark Chamberlain: pages 26, 63, 88, 137, 194, 208
Charlotte Masarik: pages 9, 181, 206, 217
Charles Everts (Richard Challis Collection): page 214

The following photographs are courtesy of the Laguna Beach Historical Society: pages 8, 42, 57, 121, 198

Preface

Coming to Laguna Beach in 1955 changed my life. Gone was the sharp-elbowed contact sport of New York City. Now I had a sort of laissez-faire in Laguna—though not entirely. Bonnie and I crossed Forest Avenue mid-street on our first day and a police officer stopped us. What had we done wrong? We had jaywalked.

Jaywalking was a way of life in New York. You could not exist without it. You'd starve to death waiting for a light to change or traffic to ease. Instead you wove your way among snarling cabbies and screeching brakes. You jaywalked. How else get anywhere?

The traffic cop asked us where we lived. We told him we'd lived a half day in Laguna Beach and before that in New York City. "Oh," he said, "that explains it." He tore up the ticket.

I worked at my typewriter all morning. I swam in the Pacific all afternoon. I slept all night. I was born for the second and final time when I hit Laguna, and Laguna caressed me. It has been a love fest.

I met Bud Desenberg late that year. He published the *Laguna Beach Post*, together with John Weld, who wrote a column for it and managed the Ford dealership in town. John could do all this because he had once been a Hollywood stunt man. Bud Desenberg lived off family money in a tiny town just north of Laguna, Corona del Mar. What Bud wanted was to remake Laguna into a boating town. He wanted to turn our beachfront into a place for countless sailboats and yachts to bob in tightly crammed slips. He was marina-crazy. He wanted Laguna Beach to be Newport Beach.

Pretty soon Bud had me writing play reviews for the *Post*. To say that these plays were less than professional would be kind. Usually they were what one would expect of an amateur production. The actors were—let's face it –a motley crew who did not realize how motley they were, and I wouldn't say so in my reviews. I invented a code. You know—"The ingenue had experience with such roles," which meant she was old enough to be my grandmother.

After a spate of such reviews I asked Bud to let me try a column. He hesitated. I was already too controversial. I was a liberal Democrat in a conservative Republican town. Republicans outnumbered Democrats by three to one. Play reviews were one thing. An opinionated column was another.

I suggested a pseudonym. Bud brightened. I had a column. Or Woody Cove had a column. Nobody knew the true identity of Woody Cove except Bud and editor Betsy Rose and Bonnie and me. But then the *Post* entered my column under my name in the annual Orange County Press Club awards competition. I won for best column, and the jig was up. My cover was blown. And nobody canceled a subscription to the *Post*.

That is how this book was born. I wrote columns for the *Post* from mid-1961 to early 1964 for five dollars a column until one day I demanded a raise and Bud in a burst of generosity boosted me to six dollars. I said to my friend Phil Interlandi, whose "Lagunagrins" cartoons gave the *Post* spice and a wry look at stuffed shirts and tourists, "Guess who's getting six dollars now." Phil had been paid five dollars per weekly cartoon. He lifted an eyebrow. "Not me," he said. "I'm getting ten." A few columns later, I quit.

I wrote columns for the *Village Sun,* and then began a hiatus. I had become too busy. I produced a book and twenty or thirty magazine pieces a year. I wrote book reviews for the *New York Times*. I wrote environmental pieces, one of which helped keep hydroelectric dams out of the Grand Canyon and another of which helped persuade the Disney Company not to turn Mineral King into a typical Disney resort. I wrote a biography of Sandy Koufax that went fourteen printings. I covered the last game Stan Musial played. I interviewed Diana Rigg backstage at the Old Vic in London. Time flew.

Our daughter, Laurel, grew up. Bonnie went back to school and later became a psychotherapist. I taught writing classes all over. Our dog, Cleo, chased rabbits almost to the day she died at age sixteen. We had two cats. Or they had us. Each lived to age seventeen. My hair turned white. We stopped high-rise development on Laguna's beaches and throughout the town. Village Laguna was born in 1971. "Laguna charm" and "village atmosphere" became vital parts of the town's vocabulary.

In 1991 Bonnie and I joined the Peace Corps, I in my seventieth year, she in her sixty-fifth. (Yes, the Peace Corps has age restrictions; you have to be at least eighteen.) We served in a tiny coffee-growing town in Costa Rica—eight hundred people, one passenger car. After our two-year stint ended, we stayed and built a house and found peace and serenity among our Tico friends. After five years, I grew homesick for Laguna. We came back, and I wrote more columns and stood at the lectern in the City Council chambers and made trouble.

Some of the columns in this book astound me. I never knew how condescending I had become toward women. I hope I have grown some since. Names of people I wrote about are a fog in my memory bank. Faces are a blank. But I do recall selecting our steaks at the Sandpiper and grilling them over an open fire, all for less than two dollars. I never ate a better steak. I argued in print with Bud Desenberg over a possible marina. I wrote about the threat of a freeway that would have ripped apart our downtown. That battle lasted years. I proposed placing our power lines underground fifty-plus years ago. We're still fighting that fight. I reported with sadness and anger that a homeless man had broken a window to gain entrance to the Resource Center shelter and in the process cut his hand and bled to death. All he had wanted was a roof over his head.

These columns are my life here in Laguna, one man's journey over the past half century.

Writing the columns was one thing. Putting them together in this book is another. My friend and wonderful editor Barbara Metzger went through all my columns, more than 200 of them. She selected these. In all the years I've worked with her, we have argued once, over one word. She was right. Rosemary Boyd designed the book and the cover and knows the world of new publishing better than anyone I have ever met. My elegant friend Charlotte Masarik shot the cover photos. Bonnie Hano—wife, lover, friend, best critic—has been next to me for all this life and all these words.

Finally, I owe my inspiration to the people of this town, who more than anything have kept Laguna Laguna. I salute you.

Hello.

1

Hello There, by Woody Cove

Laguna Beach Post, 1961–1963

August 10, 1961

Why a Pen Name *[i.e., Woody Cove]*? Why not? If it was good enough for Mark Twain, George Sand, Stendhal, O. Henry, George Eliot, and Broz, to say nothing of Gorgeous George and Marilyn Monroe, it's good enough for me. You judge a painter by his paintings, a carpenter by his carping, and a columnist by the number of names he can drop in a stick of type. Me, I dropped my own name. Let's leave it at that.

Hello.

Not that I don't like names. Names fascinate me. The other week a Laguna girl named Husband got married. Not a single local editor headlined the item "Husband Takes Groom." That's discipline.

Laguna's full of great names. We have a Gregory and a Peck, a Graves and a Coffin, a Gee and a Wiss. Even a Dixon and a Yates. Man named Combs is a landscape gardener. Girl named Musick works for an audio shop. We used to have a Synk; now we have a Leak. There's an accountant named Frame and an oil exec named Goodspeed. Man named Crum used to be a tax collector around here; guess he's picked up and gone. We have a Tilt and a Stoops, a Cash and a Cary, a Dunn and a Bradstreet, a Hipps and a Lipp, a Guy and a Doll. We also have Klass.

After having read the local rave reviews of summer stock for years now and, having seen most of the productions, I've always wondered whether the critic and I saw the same play. Finally been tipped off. It seems the reviewer has a special code: when he says something, you have to know what he really means. Here are some quotations from recent reviews, and what the drama critic actually meant:

"She has a low, well-modulated voice." *(Can't be heard past row C.)*

"This is a fun play." *(Brainless as a TV commercial.)*

"Except for an occasional line-fluff, the cast was letter perfect." *(Who threw away the second act?)*

"It's a pleasure to see such seasoned performers." *(Imagine a 60-year-old bag playing an ingénue.)*

"Director Kurt N. Kall has ruthlessly disciplined his devoted cast." *(The director showed up twice during rehearsals, and was sober both times.)*

"The capacity audience enjoyed itself immensely." *(By actual count, there were 16 spectators, 12 of them in on free passes. The other four were looking for a bowling alley, and wandered in by mistake.)*

"The play's moody atmosphere was accentuated by low-key lighting." *(Couldn't see a thing.)*

"...a witty, worldly, sophisticated comedy." *(Everybody drinks.)*

A columnist is a person of prejudices. Here are some of my current not-quite-two-cents' worth: Either the paintings at the Festival get better every year, or my taste gets worse. Probably the latter....If the state continues to insist on building its Freeway through Laguna, we ought to meet the builders up around Crystal Cove with baseball bats....Nobody has yet explained satisfactorily why a magazine like *Coronet*, with over 3-million monthly circulation and ads, has gone bust, while *Pageant*, with 600,000 monthly readers and no ads, makes oodles of money....If Dick Nixon becomes governor of California, he won't run for president in 1964, but will in 1968....New York humor is more sarcastic than California humor....I'll bet you a dime Laguna passes its next school bond....If we followed the U.S. Constitution as originally written by our Founding Fathers, we wouldn't be allowed to vote for U.S. Senators....I wish somebody would define "obscene," "smut," and "pornography" to my satisfaction....If Marilyn Monroe remarries Joe DiMaggio, it will set back the reading of Dostoievsky twenty years....You call 'em meter maids: I call 'em lady cops.

August 17, 1961

Nobody influenced more people in his own time than
Ernest Hemingway. This is a strong statement, but I
believe it is true. Shakespeare's influence was greater, of
course, but mainly on people who came later. The same
with other great men. The world is about three billion
strong, today, and whatever words are written and
read, the Hemingway mark is on them. He took a florid
artificial language and cut it to the bone, and even if you
disapprove of his arrogant males and deplore his taste
for violence, you have to admire the firm leanness of his
style.

Everybody has his favorite Hemingway and his
most despised Hemingway. I (and this is a minority
view) hate *The Sun Also Rises* and thrill to *To Have and
Have Not.* The first is gloomy, fatalistic, and unpar-
donably anti-Semitic. The other is Hemingway's affir-
mation of the brotherhood of man: no man alone stands
a blanketey-blank bloody chance. You could almost hear
Hemingway muttering those words while he held his
12-gauge shotgun in his meaty hands the other recent
morning, this big bear of a man who absolutely ruled
the world of letters, one of the last great rugged individualists, yet knowing somehow that whatever it is that
any of us wants to do, it can't be done alone.

Baffled?

I baffle easily. Confusion seems to be my normal state of
mind. For months now I've been worrying about a sign
on Harbor Boulevard: "Walter's Chow Mein, Minnesota
Recipe." It's got me so bewildered I can hardly sleep
nine hours a night. I'm afraid to ask Mr. Walter what it
means. Suppose it means what it says? All I can picture
is satisfied patrons coming out, egg roll on their faces,

and saying, "Darned clever, these Minneapolites."

That's my number-one baffle right now. I've managed to get over another baffle. This was a sign on Rosemead Boulevard, between the Santa Ana and the San Bernardino Freeways. It reads: "Family Liquor Store." Please. Don't explain it. I've learned to live with it.

Personal Prejudices

If there's a better eating experience in Orange County than the hot pastrami sandwiches at Brown's Bakery and Delicatessen on West 4th Street in Santa Ana, I haven't found it....I hate mockingbirds....It's not the humidity, it's the heat....The Pageant of the Masters was, as usual, a splendid production, but the commentary was hopelessly corny and the music even worse than usual.

People tell me I'm too negative. Think Big, they say. Be Positive. Look for the Silver Lining. So I try. I smile at people in the street. I say hello to policemen. I write friendly letters to Jimmy Utt. But then I press my luck. I was walking along the other day and Eiler Larsen said: "Hello there. How are you-oooo?" Ah-ha, I thought to myself, here is your opportunity. "Fine, thank you," I said firmly, "and how are you?" and Larsen said: "Don't start an argument with me."

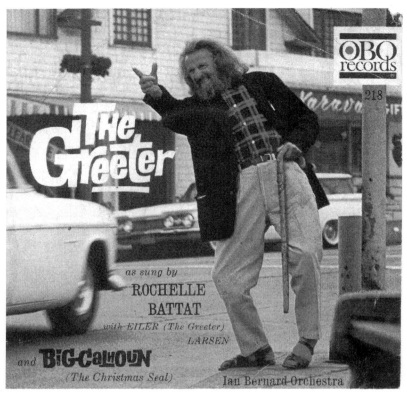

The Greeter

as sung by
ROCHELLE
BATTAT
with EILER (The Greeter)
LARSEN

and BIG-CALHOUN
(The Christmas Seal)

Ian Bernard Orchestra

OBO records

218

Eiler Larsen, the Laguna Beach "Greeter"

August 24, 1961

Laguna Marina? Phooey!

When you get down to it, the thing that makes Laguna Beach the loveliest town most of us have ever seen is the sweep of unimpeded ocean front. Tawny crescents of beach, white humpbacked surf, and a huge expanse of water meeting the sky. Boat towns are nice enough, I guess, but we've got one above us and another half-masted one down at San Clemente. It's the artificiality of them that gags me. Man-made wharfs, sheltered man-made rectangular shallow pools for anchoring, a thin scum of oil slick on the water, and people in yachting hats. And worst of all the establishment of a social hierarchy, with its snobbish boat clubs setting the pace.

"Tawny crescents of beach, white humpbacked surf, and a huge expanse of water meeting the sky"

All we ask down here is a plea for simplicity. Sure, the sight of a white sail on a glinting sapphire sea gives me a catch in the throat. But the sight and smell of a few hundred boats cluttered together, bumping against rotting piles, gives me a pain elsewhere. What it gets down to is this: A man walking into the ocean, without fins or spear guns or snorkels, unaided by sails or motors or even surfboards—that's glorious. Puny man breasting giant ocean. Can't we ever leave well enough alone?

Talking about Newport Beach, I see our neighbor up the coast has proclaimed the week of August 28–September 1 as "Anti-Communist Week" in that town.

How come just a five-day week? If a thing's worth doing at all, it's worth doing well. Newport is a pretty big community, up 'round 28,000. According to the FBI, there are some 18,000 Communists in this country. That's out of a national population of 180 million. About one Communist for every 10,000 humans. In other words, Newport Beach has two Communists and four-fifths of another one. You see why it's going to take at least a seven-day week up there? You ever try catching four-fifths of a Communist?

But what's worse is what happens if those 2.8 Communists decide to use the breathing space next weekend and make a break. Sure as blazes, if they're Commies with any taste at all, they'll head this way. And with our population of 9,000, we've already got nine-tenths of a Communist, ourselves.

There's a solution, of course. After Newport's August 28–September 1 Anti-Communist Week, we ought to have a Laguna ACW from September 4 to September 8. Then Dana Point, September 11–15, San Clemente, 18–22, Oceanside the next week, and right on down through San Diego. Maybe we'll give San Diego two weeks. You see the pattern? We'll drive all 63 Communists across the border, into Tijuana. Serve 'em right.

You might have been miffed at the Bank of America open house the other evening because the girls at the door didn't want to give away those coin candies to everybody and the lady with the free ballpoint pens made herself scarce, but I liked it. When a bank starts playing Santa Claus, all I can think of is: that's my money they're tossing away. Attaboy, B of A, hang on to it! Penny candy saved is a penny candy earned, I always say.

September 14, 1961

You are about to be privy to what we fellows in the newspaper game (and you have to call it a game, what with the salaries they pay) call a "circulation gimmick." My boss, with the initials B.D., and I will now stage round 3 of what innocently began as a mildly bigoted statement on my part that I didn't much like the idea of a marina here in Laguna. B.D. (round 2) did like the idea. So he and I will whip up a debate, the main purpose to get readers into a froth of interest so that they will call each other names at meetings and a whole flaming issue takes the whole town by storm. The result ought to be the sale of three or four extra copies of the next few papers. Maybe five, if all my relatives keep their promise.

It would not be possible, or polite, to annihilate all of B.D.'s arguments in one column, because that would end the debate, and we'd have to fish up another issue. So I'll just carry B.D. a couple of rounds (the way Nixon carried Kennedy) and take him apart piecemeal. B.D. says it's a shame we've got no place here in Laguna for the kids to launch their little dinghies and that such an experience would make men out of tykes.

Balderdash, and other assorted four-letter words. If a boy's going to be a man, he'll make it with or without dinghies (whatever in Newport they are). Think of all the Iowans who never set eyes on a marina. Yet they came out here and launched Long Beach.

B.D. (Big Dinghy, I guess) goes on to say, "In a democracy there should be room for the people with money and yachts as well as for the rest of us hoi polloi." This is known as knocking down a straw sailor. Look here, Big Dinghy, I'm for democracy. I'm even for yachts and money. I'm the last person to tell the people with yachts and money to go to Russia or New York or somewhere equally grim. Who knows, maybe someday an underage rich girl with a yacht will invite me aboard, and I'll be famous as Errol Flynn. Or somebody with money will give me some.

What Big Dinghy worries about is what should rich people do in Laguna if we don't let them have a marina. (Gosh, that is a problem.) For one thing, they can go up to Newport and make pretty little patterns of oil scum on the water up there. Then, when they're tired of soiling (oops, I mean sailing), they can drive back here and rest on our beach. Of course, they face the possibility of getting tar on the bottoms of their feet and elsewhere. But that's life. Sail a yacht in Newport and watch the oil deposits end up on Laguna's sand and eventually on my living-room rug.

To each his own, I say. Newport is a boating town. Oh, I know Newport wasn't a boat town when God made it, but then neither was Laguna a beach town. It's the way we've evolved: Newport toward boats at piers, standing like so many swaying fingers pointed by drunken sailors at the sky, and Laguna like an open face toward the sea, where a tired middle-aged man can ride a few waves and float on his back, with never a fear a motorboat will slice him in two or the guy at the starboard of a yacht will spill an iced drink down his trunks.

At least, that is what the issue ought to boil down to: people who want a town the way it is to stay the way it is (on one side) and (on the other side) people who want to destroy its evolution and hustle it off to a different size, shape, and smell.

And if that were the issue, as it ought to be, and a poll were held of all people, rich yacht-owners and poor bike-riders alike, I am confident that the marina would be voted down. I would even be so foolhardy as to place a dime bet with Big Dinghy on the result.

Unfortunately, even in a democracy, things like this have a habit of being decided by a few shrewd people who come up with words like "progress" and "make a man out of him" and "in a democracy" and who know all about variances and who can float a bond neater than most men can float a paper boat. And presto, after a few meetings, at which it will be proved we can make a couple of bucks out of the project, the contractors who are really behind the whole idea will rip and tear, spilling cement and asphalt and driving great wooden piles into the ocean floor, and we'll have a little marina, tucked out of sight—so Big Dinghy says—of all boat-haters.

But not out of sight of some Laguna-lovers.

No, honey, it doesn't mean that once we get a marina, Harry Bridges automatically takes over.

September 28, 1961

Carla, who ought to have been a tall willowy brunette with swivel hips and purple lipstick but instead was a raddled, shrieking madwoman, has made her entrance into the world and her unlamented exit, and we are many letters down the alphabet in mankind's struggle against natural disaster. But like most storms, even this bloodthirsty, man-hungry vixen had her virtues.

She ripped a half a million people out of their homes, sent them scurrying onto clogged dirt roads, a mass of struggling, straggling humanity, babies in arms or strapped to backs, people clasping old torn photos and keys to long-lost valises and frightened cats, headed for the next town, or the next, or the next, or wherever they might find a place high and reasonably dry and out of the range of Carla's maniacal laugh.

And when they got where they got—the tide of humankind, a half-million weak—the people who received them received them with open arms, with food, with milk, with diapers, with bedding, and with love.

No civil-defense authorities had warned the townspeople ahead of them to pack a gun; nobody suggested that this would be a horde of vultures descending on them. All they said to the townspeople who lived in places remote from Carla was "Here come some strangers. They're in trouble."

Faces must be red in Riverside County and in Nevada, these days, and consciences sore. But the rest of us sleep easier; Carla has turned us into human beings again. We know for certain that if a bomb drops tomorrow night, and we are thrown out on strange dark roads, there will be a haven ahead. Or if we are the haven, we know how to act. Carla—and the people of Texas and Louisiana—showed us.

The new changes in bylaws of the Festival of Arts Association—passed by a whopping 218-to-8 vote—take us further away from the old town hall idea of local government, and I deplore the trend. No longer may a person sitting at a meeting of the Festival make a nomination from the floor. Now you've got to go out, like any politician, and get 15 members' signatures on a nominating petition before you, or the man you're doing this for, can run for office on the Festival board.

This is the smooth, cool, imperturbable Organization Man approach, the no-last-minute-surprises approach: a man wants to run, he steps out and runs. It is an approach that also runs roughshod over those people without quite the strong ego (I almost said "conceit"), the positive personality (I almost said "arrogance"), to go around soliciting signatures. It also ignores that quiet, puzzled woman in the next to last row who will listen to the names of those nominated and suddenly conclude in an act of decisiveness that surprises even herself that she knows a better person than any of those named. So up she pops and presents the name.

Nothing wrong with it, and quite a bit in its favor. Now it's outlawed. Now you comb your hair and, like Willy Loman, go out with a shoeshine and a pen that writes right through the oil of a smile, and you sell yourself, or some friends. And why not, they say. It works with soap and brushes and insurance. Why not sell people the same way?

This, too, is called progress.

October 5, 1961

Wanna Join?

Art Ryon, in the *Los Angeles Times* the other day, says he's never seen a Brigitte Bardot movie, or been to someplace in Hollywood called P.J.'s. Welcome to the Never Club, Ryon. The Never Club was founded by Colonel Lemuel Q. Stoopnagel, of the Stoopnagel and Budd radio team, circa 1930, and its charter member was one of the great never-men of all time. Stoopnagel, for instance, never lifted the lid of a post office box a second time to make sure his letter had slid down. That takes restraint. I became a member when I was the only kid on the block who could eat one salted peanut and stop right there. Try it sometime.

There are a few ground rules to joining the Never Club. You've got to say Las Vegas, never just Vegas. It's Sunset Boulevard, never the Strip. You never use the word "dichotomy," especially if you know what it means.

After that, you have to come up with your own list of nevers. As for me—like Ryon—I've never seen a Brigitte Bardot movie (and you never call her BB, just as you never call Marilyn Monroe MM), and I've never been to P.J.'s either. I don't even know what P.J.'s is (or are). I've never seen an Ingmar Bergman movie, or an Ingemar Johansson one. I've never seen Elvis Presley, Pat Boone, Dick Clark, Fabian, or Tuesday Weld (and I never hope to be one). I've never seen Jayne Mansfield. I've never seen a Glenn Ford movie or a Jerry Lewis movie. I've never read a book by Lawrence Durrell or finished a poem by T. S. Eliot. I never saw Liberace or Jack Webb. I've never seen a Gina Lollobrigida film (but

I hope some day to rectify this omission. That isn't being a never-man, but simply a jerk).

The Never Club boasts quite a distinguished crowd. Latest to join is ex-President Eisenhower. (We never call him President any more, and it's automatic expulsion if you call him General; Ike is preferred.) You remember the other day he was on that charity gambling yacht, and Eva Gabor kept following him around, saying: "Isn't he vunderful?" until Ike finally said to Mamie: "Who's that?"

That's prime never-ism, when you don't recognize a beautiful blonde like Eva Gabor.

The fatal flaw in both the extreme wings of politics, other than a complete lack of a sense of humor, is an almost hysterical fear of criticism. There was no reason in the world for a few newsstands here in Laguna to keep the September 26 *Look* off the racks just because the magazine ran an uncomplimentary profile on Robert Welch and his John Birch Society. When you do that, you wipe out freedom of choice and make your bed with the totalitarian boys.

It Had to Happen

In England, they've discovered that cows give much more milk if they're permitted to watch television in their stalls. For Lagunans who find it hard enough to get any ordinary channel, much less the English Channel, I've managed to work up a list of programs most in demand by cows these days. A sort of Knudsen rating, you might call it.

One of the more popular panel shows is "I've Got a Beef." Right up there, too, is that giveaway quiz programme "Heifer or Nothing." They like the night-time roundup of current events "Moos in Review." Of the action-adventure dramas, most favored is "Danger, People Crossing."

And Number 1 continues to be "John's Udder Wife."

October 19, 1961

Ah, Civilization!

This past Sunday—according to the advertisement in
the *Los Angeles Times*—a man was to have wrestled a
bull with his bare hands, and to the death, in a Tijuana
bullring. I don't know how it all came out, but I'll tell
you I'm rooting for the bull. It was over fifteen hundred
years ago that they outlawed gladiatorial contests in
Rome as "barbaric." Haven't we come a long way since!

Noel Coward's new musical on Broadway lets loose
a blast against American kids. As Coward sees them,
they're an unruly mob, products of a permissive theory
that spurns the rod and spawns the hot rod. For all
I know, Coward is dead right (although it would be
the first time), but isn't this a case of the teapot calling
the kettle nahsty? On the stage at the Playhouse these
weekend nights you can get a long look at the products
of Eton and Harrow, where British lads are paddled into
maturity. And what a cruddy crew they turn out to be! I
don't like rudeness in kids any more than does Coward,
and I agree that discipline is fine tonic for the soul, but
if I have to choose between the teenage delinquents of
America and the adult delinquents of England, you'll
have to forgive me if I stick by our unruly mob.

Thinking Out Loud

How's about building that Freeway right through the
new hotels on the beach?...If those generals were talking on the liberal side of the issue, wouldn't the right-
wingers be screaming for them to be muzzled?...It

makes as much sense to select a stocks-and-bonds man to be the new postmaster as it would to pick a letter-carrier to take over Dean Witter....I miss those once-a-week $1.75 steak specials some Laguna restaurants used to feature every winter....If you're looking to beautify the city streets, instead of hanging flowers on power poles, why not start putting power lines beneath the ground?

His First Name Was Joe...

That's the way a full-page ad for the Jos. Schlitz Brewing Company begins; you probably saw it in the *L.A. Times* the other day. Strangest ad ever. The copy tells us Jos. Schlitz did not found the beer company. All he did was marry the widow of the man who did; then Jos. went out and got himself drowned, in water yet, in the Irish Sea. For this, they named the company after him. If the trend keeps up, we may have a whole ream of new folk heroes: the office boy who doesn't do a lick of work but cozies up to the boss's daughter; the teller's wife who shows her husband how to handle two sets of books; the guy who bleeds to death in one of those television commercials trying to prove which blade shaves you fastest.

No, thanks; I'll have a Burgey.

October 26, 1961

Sam Rayburn

I think the doctors in attendance have cheated Sam Rayburn, not telling him that the thing inside him was a cancer. Forget the word "incurable." We're all incurable, from the moment we're born. Nothing will stop us in our plunge for the grave; the wonder always ought to be that we get away with our brief little spasm as long as we do. I may be wrong, and it may well be that when my time comes (as they say) I'll also want to be kidded along. But I don't think so. I think I'll want to know what it is that's gnawing away at me, and what my chances are of prolonging a losing battle from the start. I understand that with some people this little white lie ("just a touch of lumbago…heartburn…constipation") keeps them going and that the raw truth might so depress them that they'd quit. But Sam Rayburn! A man who's wrestled with the weightiest problems of our time and somehow managed to barrel through a solution so many times that the word most often used was "a miracle." Good bills, bad bills, liberal ones, conservative ones. Ones with no chance at all, and ones with clear sailing. Hostile forces and friendly. He faced them all. A little malarkey here, a little watering down there, a batch of conditional clauses throughout, but let's get the damned bill through, boys. That was the way Rayburn operated.

And when he came face to face with the toughest bill of all, the one bill with no chance of winning, they cheated Sam Rayburn and wouldn't let him know. You think he would have quit? I think he would have spit on his palms and gone to work. Instead, they bottled this one up in the Rules Committee, and Rayburn never got his chance to meet this one, face to face, out on the floor.

No Through Street

I'd like to suggest a truce in the battle between Laguna and the State Division of Highways. A real, long cooling-off period. Say, for twenty years. We promise to stop writing letters to Sacramento, if the state stops planning to ram through its Freeway.

I'm serious. I understand that if nothing is done about a Freeway or about widening the Coast Highway in the face of an expected population increase, our traffic will be slowed to a crawl, and bumper-to-bumper conditions will prevail.

Fine. If it gets as bad as that, people who insisted on coming here in the face of such a predicted situation will have to make a choice. Get out. Give up cars for bicycles. Or walk.

I know that this isn't Progress. But then neither is the deliberate murder of a town.

Last Chance

Next Tuesday we vote for or against our children. Not quite two million bucks, spread out over the years, for new classrooms, new laboratories, new athletic fields, new bus barns, new sites for future schools. Down in Capistrano, where they built a school for 200 students and now have 600, and where Quonset huts catch the overflow, as though children were something that leaks, like rusty rainwater, they've just voted down a seventh school bond in three years. Here, our record is not quite as bad, but almost. Still, I don't know how the schools are in Capo; I don't know whether they've learned that the way you get good schools is to turn out good students under any conditions at all. In Laguna, we've learned that one. We've turned the corner. Our curriculum gets better and richer all the time. The curriculum wouldn't suffer much (not until later on, anyway) if the bond is beaten. But that's not the question. The question is how much do we think our children are worth? What price can we put on a fresh inquisitive mind, given room to roam? That's what we're voting for: room, air, and a world of learning. A ticket to the Moon, perhaps. A flight to the stars. A passport to the soul. A knowledge of our brothers.

Recently, a boy was hurt in a car accident, and his brain ruined. They awarded this vegetating child $400,000. One brain equals $400,000, the jury decided. What a bargain we're getting, then: school facilities to handle over a thousand brains, for less than two million bucks.

November 2, 1961

Laguna Charm

What's it mean? It's an expression I use, you use, we all use. Laguna charm. Do any two of us mean the same thing?

Interlandi's real estate agents mean houses with decaying roofs. People passing through mean Larsen on the street corner. Up in L.A., they mean an unemployed actor holding a homestead to the whole beach. To the rest of the world, we're the place that puts through phone calls to Peoria when we've got nothing better to do.

Put 'em together, and do they spell charm? I dunno. What I like about Laguna is wearing zoris...the smell of eucalyptus nuts...walking into Gene's Market and hearing a radio playing an aria from *Madame Butterfly*...streets with names like Glomstad Lane, Fen Way, Crabbe Way, Hinkle Place, Through Street, Bent, Goff (but not Glenneyre, Catalina, Ocean Way, Jasmine)...standing near the top of Bluebird Canyon when the rest of the town is foggy...houses that are all colors, all sizes (mostly little), all shapes (mostly cockeyed), on streets without sidewalks . . the sagging curtain at the Playhouse... Pyne Castle, the Halliburton house, the old Dickerman house...the long stretch through green fields when you leave the Freeway at the Laguna Canyon exit and head home again...coming the other way, and seeing the El Morro trailer park beach, on 101A...the acid honesty of Carl Gilbert...the dog who mooches politely at the south-end Page Boy drive-in...the sounds on Friday night when Laguna scores a rare touchdown...the old man who eats his lunch on a bench outside the library... the good-natured distrust of Easterners, Democrats, and neckties...people who don't lock their doors at night...

the children's art at the Festival…the indignation of people who don't want to buy an organ (and presto, it's bought)…the flower in Bill Martin's buttonhole…the sight of Larsen trudging home at night.

Charm? I dunno. But it describes Laguna to me.

Laguna Charm: 1920's Murphy-Smith Bungalow, now home of the Laguna Beach Historical Society

You Can Bank on It

Ocean Avenue used to have the sleazy look of streets where buses stop over. Now it's becoming *the* Laguna street. No sooner had the Bank of America put up its windowless edifice on the corner of Ocean and Beach (now aren't those silly names?) so that when you ride down Glenneyre, instead of seeing Mystic Hills, you see the B of A sign, than Laguna Federal decided it needed a new address. True, it just moved a few doors along Ocean, but, ah, what a change! Now it's a bank (so all right, it's not really a bank, it's just a place you put your money in, they save it for you and you get interest, or else you borrow money and they get interest)—now it's a bank with a fountain in the middle, and New Orleans latticework and balconies on the outside.

Ocean Avenue is rapidly becoming what Madison Avenue calls a showcase. Instead of taking your friends to the usual tourist-type haunts, like Top of the World, or sneaking into Emerald Bay without a pass, now you can take them up and down Ocean. Bankers' Row, we calls it. What's worst is that at noon, all the bankers (you can tell 'em by the watch fobs at their vests) converge on Buzan's restaurant and get together, the way conspirators used always to get together at a certain Paris café and plot to overthrow the world. I don't mind so much that they're figuring out ways to get the rest of my money. It's just that a non-banker can hardly get a place at the lunch counter any more, and eat that good sauerkraut.

December 7, 1961

Remember?

Do you remember what you were doing twenty years ago today? I remember bits and pieces of it. It was a Sunday, and I was lazing about the house, as I still do on Sundays, half-listening to a professional football game. There was an interruption, and the announcer said: "I have a flash. Japanese planes have bombed Pearl Harbor."

Today, in all those novels that recreate the day, the hero always says, "Honey, do you know what this means?" The wife nods, white-faced, unable to speak. "War," he says grimly. "It means war." And the wife sobs against his shoulder.

Well, if I had been the hero, I'd have said, "Where's Pearl Harbor?" Mainly, I was concerned about the ball game. As a matter of fact, the thing I remember best of that day was how miffed the play-by-play announcer was. After a second flash, the announcer said with obvious irascibility: "Now maybe we can get back to the ball game without any more of these interruptions."

I got to see Pearl Harbor, a year or so later. By then I knew where it was, not that it mattered, because I wasn't steering the ship. The Japanese had by this time become "Japs" or "Nips" or "yellow-bellied so-and-sos." The only good one was a dead one. Tojo had long yellow fangs.

In our outfit we had posters showing the differences between Chinese and Japanese. One of them had more body hair; it must have been the Japanese because political cartoonists compared them to monkeys. If you saw an Oriental with body hair, you shot first and asked questions later. Nobody explained what the Japanese would be doing, fighting with their clothes off, so we

28

could see their body hair. The only Japanese soldier I ever saw had all his clothes on. He was asleep on a hill, about thirty or forty feet above me. I was alone, and he was alone, and neither one of us had any guns, so we couldn't make good Japanese or good Americans out of each other. I went back down the hill and reported what I had seen, and later a squad of soldiers, with guns, went up the hill. They came back down with him, alive, a prisoner.

Arnold Hano, 2nd from right, being inducted into the army.

That's what I remembered most about Pearl Harbor. I remember that I had been ashamed that I had not charged up the hill and captured the prisoner myself. Today I am glad that I hadn't. Things change. Today the Chinese are Commies, and the Japs are Japanese again.

And I wonder what it will be like in another twenty years?

Empathy or Sympathy?

Harry Golden has a new crusade. He's against the use of the word "empathy." What's wrong with old-fashioned "sympathy" he wants to know. Nothing. Oh, there may be a little difference; elementary psych students use "empathy" to mean feeling exactly the way the other fellow feels (a total impossibility), not just feeling sorry for him. But there's a more valid reason why we can't give up "sympathy" for "empathy." What would the ultra-conservatives use for a term, then? You just can't say, "He's a Com-emp." It doesn't have the vigor of "Com-symp": it doesn't have the great advantage of "symp" sounding exactly like "simp." Let's hope Harry Golden wins this one. Not only is our vocabulary at stake, but so too may be our Moral Fiber.

Payola

Talking about moral fiber, I've just about given mine up for the duration. Couple of weeks ago I praised a cartoon by Frank Interlandi. Now Frank's given me the original. It opens up a whole world of possibilities. I can stop knocking and start boosting. Who knows, if I say I like a chair in Baker's window, maybe they'll give it to me, or at least invite me in to sit in it a time or two. Or if I praise a surrealistic painting, maybe Mark Engleman will give it to me for free (wrapped in plain brown paper, of course).

You call it payola. I call it gratitude. That's what made America strong.

"Martha, Do you have anything you want to say before the baseball season starts?" Cartoon by Frank Interlandi's twin brother, Phil.

March 15, 1962

How to Succeed Without ½ Trying

Understand, I have no real kick with the Laguna Beach schools, but sometimes I have to confess puzzlement. The other day my eight-year-old daughter came home and admitted she'd made five mistakes in a recent arithmetic test.

"Out of how many?" I asked.

"Oh, thirteen or twenty," she replied.

Then she added she'd made six errors on another exercise. Finally, to put the frosting on the Pi, she said: "And I got 11 wrong on another test."

Assuming a kid who gets 5, 6, and 11 wrong on three arithmetic tests can't add well enough to know how many she got wrong, I asked her to bring home the papers. She did, and by Geo(metry), it was 5, 6, and 11 wrong.

Two days later, she came home with another paper. Yep, you guessed it. This time it was a Mathematics Award.

Are You for It, or Are You Stupid?

The Civic League is busily preparing a series of questions to be asked of the seven candidates to the City Council and to be answered at a forum later this month, open to all. I just hope the questions are more neutrally worded than the one asked of Civic League members at the recent annual meeting, on beach control. After some fairly spirited debate on the pros and cons, chairman Paul Griem asked members to vote whether they wanted "an intelligent reasonable plan of beach control" or whether we should just go along the way we do now. Heck, nobody wants to admit he's voting against something "intelligent." I can just see the way the question might have been worded by someone on the anti-beach-plan side: "You want an unintelligent, undemocratic, greedy beach plan, or shall we continue the way we are and at the same time improve the policing, enforcing anti-litter laws, and in general regulate the offensive behavior of a few visitors who give the rest a black eye?"

Who d'you think would have won that one? No contest.

Not that there aren't lots of questions to be asked, and mighty pertinent ones, too. For instance, I'd like to pose this question to the seven candidates:

"Suppose the City Council passes a beach-control plan, and Marilyn Monroe shows up without any money and without a pass, and with a low-cut bikini? What should be done? (You have, here, a multiple-choice: a) Immediately waive the cover charge; b) Declare Laguna a disaster area and invoke emergency measures; c) Blow up the City Council.)

I think a city councilman ought to be perceptive. So I'd like to know whether the candidates can tell Frank and Phil Interlandi apart and, if they can, which is which. I'd like to know how tolerant my city councilmen are: Are you for or against fog and modern art (and can you tell *them* apart)? One of our candidates said he was "proud to be part of a town with a rich artistic heritage." My question, then, is why he left and came to Laguna. Another candidate says she's against turning the beaches into a litter dump for "every Tom, Dick, and Harry with a girl, a can of beer, a surfboard, and five gallons of gas." Does that mean she's against young people, love, beer, surfing, and autos (and if so, what else is there)?

So you can see the properly phrased question can be very revealing. Of the questioner, that is.

March 29, 1962

You Want My Vote?

The average political pressure group is called a lobby. Among us artists, of course, it's an entresol, and as a vociferous entresoloist I want you to know how happy we artists are these days for the sudden attention thrust upon us by the candidates for City Council. You'd think eggheads were in season, or something.

Frankly, I don't really like it. It's scary. Couple of years ago if a man announced he was for artists, you'd have run him up to Newport on a rail, or called in an exterminator. Now we've got one candidate who actually is a writer. Another candidate keeps yelping how he wants to retain Laguna's cultural-artistic heritage, which used to be like saying you wanted to retain typhoid. And finally, we've got a sweet little housewife who is suddenly being offered to the electorate as a gal who'll take care of the interests of working artists (or so says Dixi Gail Hall, who ought to know, I guess).

What's this all mean? How does a politician look after the interests of artists? Take me. I'm an artist. I've got my Orange County Press Club card to prove it, paid through 1962. (At the end of 1962, if I were smart, I'd swap it for a plumber's union card, but then I'm not smart; I'm an artist.)

How's Mrs. Keeley or Dick Sears or George Wolfe or any of 'em going to help further my interests? Free typing? Carbon paper that actually makes a legible third copy? Changing a ribbon without getting ink under my fingernails? My interests are simple, Mrs. Keeley. All I want these days is to write a big blockbuster of a novel in thirty days, have it picked up by the Book of the Month Club and sold to the movies for $50,000.

If you can come up with a formula, I'll swallow my anti-suffragette tendencies and my foolish bias that a woman's place is in the kitchen or the bedroom and vote for you.

Or to bring it down to more mundane matters, how's about letting us writers use capital gains when we figure out our income tax? Inventors use capital gains; what's the difference? We both steal from other guys. I don't know what capital gains is (or are), but Eisenhower used it (them) when he had a book ghosted and it (they) saved him half his taxes. If Eisenhower's an artist, so am I. And so is Dixi Gail Hall.

The unfortunate answer to the whole problem is that politicians can't look out for the interests of artists. We're the last of the real rugged individualists, the last of the guys who'll take a chance on getting by without any help from the outside. You think the Utts and Shells are go-it-aloners? G'wan. They're even taking their pay from the government. The only way a politician can help an artist is to keep out of his way. Let him alone. Let him paint, write, whistle, or build without a cop or a politician or Arthur B. McQuern over his shoulder. We're the last real hope of the free enterprise, open competition system. We work alone; we ask no help, no handout. We produce or we fail. No subsidies. No fringe benefits except for a wife who keeps the kids quiet when Daddy's allegedly thinking. We punch no time clocks, beg for no coffee breaks, have no hours, pass no hat for the boss's birthday. We even occasionally achieve what scientists tell us can't be achieved. We sometimes make something out of nothing.

If Mrs. Keeley, Dick Sears, and George Wolfe really want to look after the interests of the artists of this community, there's a simple method. Just assume that artists are people.

I admit this, too, is a scary thought, but once you've accepted it, the whole problem dissolves. Say it over and over again: artists are people, artists *are* people, artists ARE people.

Gosh, Honey, what do you mean I'm protesting too much?

May 3, 1962

Holy Week

Walking down Thalia Street, from the Coast Highway to the head of the stairs leading to the beach, you could see it ahead of you, crude and faded as it was, drawn on a concrete wall with a child's hand.

A Star of David with a dagger plunged through it and the letters DEATH scrawled beneath. A few feet away, in darker, bolder lines, a Nazi swastika.

This was Thursday, April 19, Easter Week. But the desecrated Jewish star and the Nazi symbol hadn't been drawn by any of our recent out-of-town visitors. The drawings had been there at the foot of Thalia Street ever since January of this year. It was, however, the first time I had seen them.

That Thursday afternoon, the existence of the drawings was brought to the attention of the Laguna Beach police department via a phone call, in the expectation the police would take swift steps to erase the insult.

On Sunday, April 22, I walked down the same street to the same wall. The same drawings were still there. Three days had gone by, and the religious star still had a knife buried in its heart; the same Nazi swastika gloated nearby.

Three days. And what three days! Friday, April 20, had been Good Friday—God's Friday, it means the anniversary of Jesus's death. Two days later, Easter Sunday—the day of Jesus's resurrection, and the greatest day of hope of all the Christian calendar.

Three days between the phone call to the police and Easter Sunday, and no action had been taken to wipe out this foolish, stupid, barbarous obscenity.

The police were surely very busy those three days, what with the teenagers and the traffic and noisy parties and wandering drunks. But I keep thinking of those other three days over nineteen hundred years ago—the betrayal, the Judas kiss, the arrest, the swift trial, the crucifixion, the vigilance at the tomb, the empty grave, the risen figure. Perhaps the most important three days in the history of the Western world.

Of course the police were busy in Laguna Beach these recent three days. But that busy?

Mañana

I am by nature a procrastinator. I think nearly everyone is. We've just procrastinated on the beach-control plan and, I hope, killed it for a while. That's fine. I remember vividly the unanswered argument of Paul Griem of the Civic League at the unlamented "open" meeting on beach control a couple of months ago, in which Griem asked rhetorically: "Tell me, do you like Laguna Beach during Easter Week?" The implication was that the beaches became overrun by rowdies, overcrowded by visitors, and unfit for Lagunans. So this past Easter vacation I spent three days on the beach. Nobody got in the way of my bridge hand; I never interfered with their volleyball. We all had acres of room; I saw no rowdyism. Easter Week is our only really troublesome period, and it passed this time with reasonable quietude. The beaches weren't overcrowded. They weren't crowded at all. And this was the finest Easter weather we've had in the seven years I've been in Laguna Beach.

Whether the beach-control plan is workable or not, whether it is undemocratic or not, whether it is unconstitutional or not, whether it would hurt business or not no longer seems to matter. First things first. There is just no need for a restriction. Perhaps in a few years there will be. Then we can argue all the other points. Now, there's no need. We've got the answer to Paul Griem. "Yes, we like Laguna in Easter Week. The beaches, especially."

May 15, 1962

The Sound of Childish (S)laughter

The dedication of Bluebird Park has, as usual, left me a quivering mass of contradictions. I don't know whether I like it or not.

Take Opening Day. Here were all those lovely ladies who'd worked so hard and so well, and we wanted to hear of their accomplishments and of the future plans for the park. The loudspeaker didn't work. Meanwhile, a squad of El Toro marines did some snappy close-order drill, so snappy and close, in fact, that one marine hit himself on the head with his rifle butt and knocked his cap off. Even the flag didn't behave. It was run up the flagpole, but it got snarled before it reached the top, and it stood at three-quarters mast, as though not sure whether this was indeed a festive occasion or a funeral.

But the kids! They marched in beautifully, Boy Scouts and Girl Scouts and Non Scouts, and then, with patience and discipline we've been told no longer existed among our young, stood uncomplaining and unmoving for nearly an hour on the dusty sun-baked floor of the park during the unheard speeches. They even held their ranks, most of 'em, when the chow wagon pulled up with free hot dogs and other goodies, courtesy of the Elks.

When it was over, Bluebird Park was a reality. They call it Bluebird Park, of course, because there are no bluebirds, and they call it a park because there is no grass.

I have a proprietary interest in BP. (I even have a financial interest, of sorts. For a year I paid taxes on a piece of the park, even though the city owned it and should have been paying. Ah, the mysteries of escrow!) For the past couple of years I've watched from a baseball-swing away as the laborers came into the arroyo and ripped up the wild brush and sent lizards and sow bugs scurrying before the blades of their bulldozers. I watched as the tangle of gold and green and brown turned into an arid plain, a dust bowl.

The park is young, and it will improve. Right now it has a few trees and a bike path and some metal hoops that look part of a croquet game for giants. None of it is as good as the old wild tangle of brush my daughter used to disappear in, but I appreciate that there are some odd parents who prefer level playgrounds and giant croquet hoops to the possibility of stepping on a sleeping rattlesnake.

There are problems in Bluebird Park. Some of the kids use the bike path and others run about the dust bowl, but most of the kids walk to one end and slide down a rocky path to an even lower level where the brush still grows wild. There, out of sight, they play in an old drainpipe at the edge of a crumbling wall of dirt and rock. Strange, isn't it? We spend time and money and labor in ripping out the wilderness and smoothing it nice and even, and then the kids find a corner where the bulldozers couldn't reach, and that is where they play. When the rains come next winter, there could be trouble—a cave-in, a quick rush of water. You can't keep the kids out, but you can tell 'em it's not such a smart idea by putting up a fence and posting a sign or two.

Nor is that all. The main entrance to the Park is at Cress St. Cress has always been a pleasant street to drive, especially if you like potholes and hairpin curves. Beyond a hairpin these days is likely to be a kid on a bike, rushing over to the park. If we want to postpone that first awful screech of tires and the first even worse phone call to some mother, we'll have to hurry. We need a safety crossing for the kids; we could use a bike path along Cress leading to the Park; there ought to be a few warnings: CHILDREN AT PLAY, and a 15 MPH zone posted from the corner of Cress and Temple Terrace to beyond the entrance to Bluebird Knolls.

The lovely ladies have built our kids a park. Now let the rest of us make it reasonably safe.

Bluebird Park

May 24, 1962

Little League

I'm surprised and amused by the fuss raised by Boat Canyon residents over using the canyon for a future Little League field.

Back in 1956, I helped out in Little League, serving on the board of directors. It was a natural for me, you might say. As a writer, I'm used to collecting rejects. My job in Little League was to help put together what we diplomatically called a minor league, made up of kids who'd tried out for Little League and didn't make one of the regular teams. So Harvey Davis and I collected these rejects, and took 'em over to a field knee-deep in weeds, and we played ball that summer. It wasn't bad, actually; the kids seemed to have a good time. And even though there wasn't much skill, either in the managing or in the playing, we whooped it up and made up in enthusiasm and noise for the failure to hit a curve ball. Or catch one. The reason I mention it now is that the field knee-deep in weeds where we whooped it up was an empty lot on the property where the Safeway now stands.

Yep. Boat Canyon.

My Not Quite 2¢ Worth

The Festival of Arts people surely have enough money to replace that faded 48-star flag in their office with an up-to-date model....If you asked me what enterprise in the offing excites me most, I'd be torn between this summer's Festival of Opera and next season's opening production of the Community Players, *Green Pastures*. No, they're not doing it in blackface....You wouldn't think you could misspell Virgil Partch's name so many times and in so many ways as the *Post* did the other week. C'mon, gremlins, beat it....If Orange County voters don't boot Hugh Plumb out of his assessor's job on June 5, I'll be mighty surprised. Plumb's opponent is a Republican named O'Brien, and this Democrat for once is delighted to vote for the man, not the party. ... Has there ever been a more stylish daily sports column than that written by Jim Murray in the *L.A. Times*? ... The town may look beautiful these days, but wasn't that smell ghastly when our newly torn weeds got rained on and began to rot? Made a guy kinda yearn for Omaha and the old stockyards ....Those croquet hoops over at Bluebird Park have nicely turned into the zingiest swings. There's one swing that turns round and round, and if the kids would only go home, I'd take a spin.... The town fathers don't have to look very hard to find a qualified man for that city manager post. How about Jack Bergsjo?

Population Explosion

A gal named Mary Louise Grey, who lives in Los Angeles, has written the *Post* to the effect that she's decided not to move to Laguna Beach after all. Phew! Had us worried for a while. Turns out the co-ops distress her. So does the thought of the marina and freeway. We may have something here. How's about building three very garish co-ops, one on the Coast Highway just beyond Emerald Bay, another out in Laguna Canyon a few miles, and a third between South Laguna and Laguna?

That ought to frighten 'em off in droves. And don't let's tell Harold Reed—yet—we've decided we don't want his marina. Keep 'em guessing. The same with the freeway. A year or so ago we announced that our population was up to 10,000. According to a recent survey, now it's 9,800. If we can stay just ugly enough in spots, and if we hint darkly of newfangled roads and old-fangled dinghies just around the corner, maybe we'll never hit 10,000. Or, perhaps, like the white citizens' councils down South, we can provide free transportation to, say, Garden Grove for anybody who wants to stay out. Mary Louise Grey, stay home.

November 1, 1962

Never on Sunday

The meter maids are gone, and I for one miss them.
The whole problem has been a lack of communication.
I mean, how can you whistle at a cop? Put a couple
of good-looking chicks on the street, have 'em walk
around at an indolently leisurely pace, hips rolling gently, trim ankles flashing by, and there's only one conclusion a healthy red-blooded American boy can leap to.

The next thing you know, you've been arrested for
accosting a cop.

My only personal contact with the meter maids was
undoubtedly typical. I came running out of Bushard's
one day, knowing my meter time was running out with
me. Too late. There was her calling card under the wind-
shield wiper. I pulled the ticket off and went storming
down Forest Avenue and caught up with her a few cars
away. I was about to make the usual alibis: "I ran out of
change, the damn meter clock is running fast, I contrib-
ute money to the policewoman's ball every year," and
the rest, when I looked at the ticket.

She'd made it out to a make of car called "Jaeger."
My car is a Renault. She called the car a '58. It's a '59.
She counted all the doors and wrote: "Two door sedan."
It's got four doors.

Patiently I pointed out these mistakes. "Come now,"
I said very gently, "I know you try hard and it's been
a very long day, but don't you think you might have
turned in a better paper?" Together we opened and shut
the doors and counted them aloud. I explained all about
the car registration on the steering column and how she
could get pertinent information from that. "But," she
said breathlessly, "isn't that breaking and entering?"

I told her I thought she'd be allowed one teensy breaking and entering, and finally I said: "Now, you don't want all those men to see how many mistakes you made, do you?"

And she burst into tears, and tore up the citation. Honest. I wanted to comfort her, but how do you let a cop cry on your shoulder?

Even the new city manager recognizes this problem. His memorandum to the City Council, announcing the impending resignation of our meter maids, cites one drawback to the use of lady cops:

"The position of female parking enforcement lacks flexibility in that they cannot be used for other work in periods of inclement weather or emergency."

Forgetting the almost-total lack of imagination on the part of the city manager, the statement is a perfect wrap-up of the situation. These women simply can't be used for other work. Can you imagine them sitting around the precinct-house on a dull evening and a regular cop saying: "How's about a hand or two of poker?" and the meter maid saying: "Goody. Which is better, two of a kind or a royal flush?"

Then there's Sunday parking. In the old days, it was free, and the meter maids could dress up in their go-to-meeting best, from floppy bonnets right on down to spiked heels, and they could close their eyes and sing "Rock of Ages."

Now they tug on their dreary beige uniforms on a Sunday and pound the old beat. The whole thing's foreign to human nature, and though we'll surely miss 'em, it is an act of mercy, firing those girls.

November 22, 1962

Thanksgiving

I'm thankful for the $1,500,000 from the state and federal governments for expansion of the Community Hospital....But I'm even more thankful that the pioneer leave-us-alone, we-don't-want-any-handout spirit of the South Coast is willing to swallow its pride and take the money.

I'm thankful the city fathers and mother agreed to donate city funds (yours and mine) to the Chamber of Commerce for Christmas decorations to make our town prettier....But I'm even more thankful to Dick Sears for voting to stick to the original figure of $2,000 instead of upping it at the last minute.

I'm thankful Orange County has a lower death rate than the city of San Francisco....But I'm glad to be able to go up to 'Frisco and die a little every so often. And I'm most thankful nobody in 'Frisco cares if you call it 'Frisco.

I'm thankful the Children's Theatre is progressing so nicely....But I'll be eternally in bondage to anybody who invites me elsewhere on December 28 and 29.

I'm thankful there aren't too many own-your-own apartment builders with the attitude of the newly opened Laguna Seacrest at 520 Cliff Drive. Families with children can't buy in.

I'm thankful people are discovering the needs of our library....But I'll be more grateful if somebody figures how to get rid of all the ants that infest the back bookshelves and make book borrowing a nippy game at best.

But I'm really most thankful we seem to have reached a hiatus on controversy, a peaceful lull (probably before a storm) during which nobody is screaming invective. The marina mob is slumbering, the indignation ilk has taken Alka Seltzer for its inner rumbles, the letters-to-the-editor columns are filled with thank-yous and poems and subscription renewals.

Come to think of it, it's a helluva note. What's wrong with everybody?

How Green Was the Valley

My wife and daughter and I went up into the hills of Bluebird Canyon this past Sunday and looked at the new houses going up, priced from $35,000 to $55,000. Rancho Laguna, they call it.

This is old hunting ground for us. My beagle dog used to disappear into these hills seven years ago and yip her way after rabbit. My daughter used to run away into these same hills, hidden by brush higher than her head. Rattlesnakes used to inhabit these slopes, but even then, seven years ago, the occasional bulldozer blades had routed most of them to less noisy, less dangerous nooks. This south wall of Bluebird Canyon is one of the truly lovely sights of this truly lovely town, a simple sweep of nature untouched by man and his yen to destroy.

Now there are a handful of houses, and the hill is beginning to be pocked. I counted fifteen houses on Sunday, but I probably missed a few. Fifteen houses make a difference. But fifteen—or twenty-five, or even thirty-five—would simply be a few pocks on this huge green face. So I asked one of the builders—a man named Davis—whether it was true that they planned to put seventy-five houses on this piece of land. He shook his head and grinned. "Nope," he said. "Not seventy-five. We're putting four hundred homes in here. This place is too valuable to leave to nature."

Our town will be able to boast in a few months that building contracts are up, the cash registers are singing, business is good.

And man's fingertip hold on beauty, his bond to nature, has been further chipped away.

Honey, that's not true. Even if I had $35,000, I wouldn't buy up there. The bedrooms are too small.

January 24, 1963

A Sun in the Place

Despite my predilection for backing losers, I've made a wild nickel bet that Velma Sun will win OPERATION OPERA. Perhaps by the time you read this, the struggle between Mrs. Sun and Sylvain Robert will have been resolved, and one of them will be putting on next summer's opera festival.

I have nothing against Robert. I'm sure he could put on a fine opera festival. I'm sure he can get a passel of big names.

But the fact is, if it weren't for Mrs. Sun there wouldn't be any struggle to put on next summer's opera festival. There wouldn't be any festival. (I'm not too sure—knowing the efficiency of Mrs. Sun—there'd even be another summer.) Very few places in the United States ever staged outdoor opera in any summer. Certainly no place as small as Laguna Beach ever dreamed of trying it. Along came Velma Sun: Presto! A stunning three weekends of beauty and creativity.

Now, Velma Sun didn't do this all by her lonesome. She tore around and in a week's time she had a board of directors. She and the board picked Sylvain Robert to be their producer. She and the board brought in Eugene Ober to conduct, and Ober fashioned a homegrown orchestra that sounded like satin. The operation snowballed, and on August 4, 1962, we had opera in Laguna Beach.

That is the issue. Before Mrs. Sun, we had no opera. With Mrs. Sun, we had opera. Now, we can still have opera, with or without Mrs. Sun. But why in Verdi's name would we kick out the woman who made all this possible? With Mrs. Sun as this year's Festival of Opera coordinator, Laguna has a priceless opportunity to put on an opera season in 1963 at least as good as it was in '62.

I don't know about you, but that's more than good enough for me.

Laguna Charm, Neon Div.

Phew, another problem solved. For years, we've lived off Cress Street—first on top of Bluebird Canyon and in more recent times near the intersection of Cress and Mountain Road—and for just as many years we'd had a devil of a time telling our out-of-town visitors how to find us. You know the routine. "Turn up Cress Steet. No, not Crest. *Cress.* You'll recognize it by Raines Market, on the corner." Well, without informing us, they changed it from Raines to Jensen's, and we had guests hitting San Clemente (which isn't a bad idea, at that) before they realized they'd missed the turnoff. When we finally got to memorize that Raines was Jensen's, it suddenly became Discount. You can imagine the havoc. Steaks got cold and drinks got warm, and my wife threatened to sue the city unless they put up a big, permanent, easily recognized sign at the corner of Cress and the Coast Highway.

Now it's taken care of, courtesy of Rancho Laguna. A great big 20-foot sign, lit up all day and half the night, on top of Discount (né Jensen's, out of Raines), and soon we'll be able to tell our guests: "Put on your dark glasses. When you get hit smack between the eyes with a sign big enough to play basketball on, and bright enough to give you a sunburn, you'll know you're there."

Say, Honey, do you think if I keep giving Rancho Laguna all this free advertising, they'll give us a house for free?

February 21, 1963

Fan Mail

Avid Reader encloses a clipping from a magazine and this note: "You think you're having typo problems, read this one." The clipping says: "One of our Midwest readers noted this item in his local newspaper: 'Our paper carried the notice last week that Mr. John Smith is a defective in the police force. This was a typographical error. Mr. Smith is really a detective in the police farce.'"

I tell you, Avid, I think you've been took. I don't believe any such item ever appeared in the unnamed paper. For one thing, us newspapermen don't use "Mr." in front of a guy's whole name. Later on, after we've identified the character, we switch to Mr. Smith, although more often it's just plain Smith. Secondly, I'm suspicious of people named John Smith. As a matter of fact, I think you made up the whole thing yourself, and if you've got nothing better to do with your time, the least you can do is stop bothering other people. In any event, Avid, you and I know that when the boys in the back room get through with the whole botched-up item, it'll come out: "polite farce." Serves you right.

Beach Restriction

Attorney-General Mosk has said Laguna can keep non-paying outsiders off some of its beaches. Mosk says he was swayed in part by the argument that health factors were at play. That an overcrowded beach, full of people and beer cans and used food containers, could be a sanitation menace.

So we solve the problem how? By letting in as many strangers as want to come, provided they pay? There is absolutely no guarantee we'll get more health. Just more money. The money, I assume, will buy more trash cans and more beach policemen. (I know just the guy for the job, too. He's named John Smith, and he's fed up to here with the town he works for. Seems the local paper called him a defective.) But even with more trash cans and more beach cops, I suggest there'll be more, not less, dirt. An out-of-towner who suddenly has to pay to get on a beach he used to get on for free is just as suddenly a man who feels he has purchased certain inalienable rights. Like drinking beer, for one. And tossing his beer can away from him, after a quick discreet look around.

Look. If we want a clean beach, and it's going to cost money, why not ask Lagunans—who are the most concerned—to pay a penny a day in some sort of new tax?

That's $36,000 a year in new revenues. That way *we'll* be buying the receptacles and paying the beach police. We'll be in charge. And whereas a visitor may be offended and indignant at a crass new tax represented by a turnstile, we will simply realize a responsibility for something we cherish. Our beaches. The attorney-general says we can, legally, restrict our beaches. But he doesn't say we have to.

But actually isn't all this talk about sanitation a smokescreen? Isn't it that we just don't want strangers on our beaches? We don't want them staining our sand? We want 'em to go back where they came from? Aren't we playing the restrictive-covenant game, of sorts? Emerald Bay doesn't let Jews and Negroes and Orientals live in their hoity-toity little corner. We won't let Anaheimites lie on the same sand that touches our pretty white chests. Isn't it all the same?

All right, Honey, let's practice. You look right, I look left. You look front, I'll look rear. Then, quick underhanded flip so beer can lands where that family is sitting. Now, look innocent. Fine.

February 28, 1963

Pyne Needling

I had never prowled through Pyne Castle until the other day, when we members of the press and other freeloaders met at the wine cellar of the Castle for a preview of the new apartments David Young is soon to throw open for you conspicuous consumers.

The wine cellar, of course, is on the second floor, which may give you some hint of the vague sprawling nature of the Castle, which no amount of modernizing and slicing into brand-new apartments can totally efface. It surely must have been something in the old days, the rooms leading on to more rooms, the cedar closets to more closets, the bathrooms seemingly by the dozens. There's a downstairs kitchen big enough to bone a whale in, with iceboxes so huge they have doors that open up the back of the icebox so you can find food you can't quite reach from the front.

But the part that intrigued me is the neglected third floor, with its trapdoors and its layer of dust and news clippings dating back to June of 1935. Even older was a penciled letter, lying on the floor. Ah, I thought, an old love letter! Or a letter reflecting on the grandeur of the Pynes, a key to the darkness that covers the origins of the family that built the Castle. A letter—I was sure—that attested to the graceful nobility of the Castle's progenitors. So I copied it all down, as any good reporter would (you call it prying; I call it intellectual curiosity), and if I'm correct in assuming the copyright laws hold only for 56 years, this tattered letter, dated May 20, 1900, is public domain, and you are entitled to glean its priceless contents.

"Pyne Music Co.

"Will send you the balance due on organ which is 50c. I got the organ for 25 dollars. Our music teacher and her husband went with us to look at it which was Mr and Mrs Brown and my self and husband. Forest Pyne let me have it with the understanding that as it was I could have it for 15 dollars or we take it and he would put in new reeds, fix it up for $10 extery. He never did it. Every time I would speak about it they would promise to come next week and so they never came. Mrs Brown did not want me to pay any more than $16 until they did as they agreed and my husband did not....I have written agreement between Forest Pyne and my self that I could have as long a time as I wanted to pay for it and a garntee that it would be keep in repair for three years. He said he needed the room for pianos, wanted to get it out of the way. So I have looked my receipts over. I owe you 50c which I will send you. I think you ought to be satified. Yours truly Mrs. W. A. James."

You may think, perhaps, this was the beginning of the Pyne fortune, this promise of fixing reeds but never delivering. Fortunately, the truth is more romantic and sustains us whenever we have doubts about the American Way. One of the Pynes sold a piano to someone, one day, and instead of taking money Pyne accepted a piece of scrubland in Santy Anny someplace, and hit oil.

Still, I am disappointed. If I ever rented one of David Young's apartments in Pyne Castle, I would find it troublesome, sleeping, worrying about Mr and Mrs W. A. James who had bought a fifteen-dollar organ and found they had paid ten dollars extery for services promised but never rendered. And I might imagine in the long upstairs ballroom where later Pynes surely danced away the elegant evenings a sound a broken organ reed might make—a wailing chord that cries out:

"Exter-yyy, exter-yyy, exter-yyy. Pyyyne, you took ten dollars exter-y from meee."

Why, yes, Honey, I suppose I would have even more trouble sleeping, what with the rents they're asking.

Pyne Castle

March 21, 1963

Spring

Spring is here. My apricot tree has already blossomed. There are tiny buds on our lime bush. The bougainvillea—which looked like a deserted rat's nest a few weeks ago—is fresh with pale green leaves. Soon it will be pink. (Anybody can have red bougainvillea.)

For me, spring began before all these manifestations. It began a couple of Sundays ago, when the Girl Scouts had another birthday.

Laurel Hano, far left, and Bonnie, back, far right

My daughter put on her Brownie uniform and I tied her orange tie, and my wife put on her leader's uniform (a redundancy, for sure), and we all went up to the Newport Harbor High School for the annual songfest that marks this birthday. Children bursting into song is a more obvious sign of a new year, new birth, new growth, nature at its loveliest.

The songfest is really an amazing performance. Here are several hundred kids, drawn from Newport, Costa Mesa, Laguna, and Corona del Mar—many of whom have never seen each other before—and without rehearsal, they sit and sing like little angels. Somebody said to me, "What do you mean, you didn't cry during the play *All the Way Home*?" Well, I didn't cry then, but my eyes are always wet listening to the Scouts sing.

These kids have some inner secret I wish they'd share with the rest of us grownups. Before the songfest begins, the Scouts and their leaders set up their displays on folding tables; other Scouts put up flags and ceremonial regalia. Then after the singing is over, the adults come down from the stands and walk around, viewing the displays, and the children keep singing for a while and eventually join their families and friends. And nobody—nobody—pushes, squeals, overturns a table, hits, knocks down a flag. The kids play, they walk, they even run around on the gym floor where all this takes place, but in the two years I've attended the show, I've yet to see a single nasty act.

Song, probably, is the immediate answer. The games we play are often based on violence and undue competition. Conversations turn into debates which turn into wrangles. Lovemaking is so often an act of triumph on one side and submission on the other. Friendships are rotted by suspicion, hostility. But when we sing together or watch and listen while others sing, there is a melting of envy and the closest thing to brotherhood I have yet witnessed.

I don't know what you plan to do on Girl Scout Birthday next year—it falls on an early Sunday in March—but if I were you, I'd mark it on the calendar right now. It makes spring more meaningful.

Sonic Blasts

Lest you think I've gone soft (or deaf), I want you to know I've also been hearing those air jockeys turning on the heat lately. Maybe the spring juices have got to the boys, too. I don't know. But I do know they've got a hell of a nerve. All right, so they're our front line against the enemy. All right, they lead a life geared to the knowledge they may die in the skies so you and I will be safe. I don't care. When I was in the infantry, I didn't go around firing my M-1 up in the air in crowded neighborhoods. There is a smug contempt these pilots are displaying, a reckless indifference to the rights of others. It is almost as though we were the enemy.

Say, Honey, where'd you put my M-1? I feel like going out and celebrating.

April 11, 1963

Gremlinology

The gremlin—my dictionary says—is a mischievous sprite imagined to inhabit airplanes and cause mishaps. Imagined, hell! They're there, all right, and not just in airplanes. We've got a few land-based gremlins, and one of the sprite-liest is right here in the back room of the *Post,* and I am hereby declaring war on him. Or her.

I didn't mind when the gremlins got into my copy and rearranged words and phrases and turned my material into something not quite as I intended. Still, any change was usually for the better. It was a bit more touchy when the gremlin invaded Arthur O'Connor's movie column, because O'Connor is a gentleman, bred to a quaint code of not swinging anything more lethal than a doeskin glove, and not even that unless your seconds exchange notes. Gremlins don't employ seconds. In any event, O'Connor and I are men, and we men can take care of ourselves.

Last week, the gremlins stepped across the line of decent mischief and became downright profane. And right in Sally Reeve's column on People, Places, and Things (which, come to think of it, doesn't leave much to the rest of us). You read it, of course, and you're probably still blushing. There was Mrs. Reeve, penning a lofty panegyric to realtor Milt Hanson (and poor Mike Jackson, holding his head, wondering what had come over the *Post,* admitting that realtors were people) and, in the midst of the encomium, a mention of Hanson's military service.

Apparently, so Sally says, Milt served in the Air Force, during which time he managed to assemble a scrapbook, in the hopes someday of landing a job in the entertainment field. (Of such grubby ambitions are great realtors born.)

Well, the gremlin leaped. Give a gremlin a foot—I always say—and he'll grab for a thigh, which leads me to conclude it's a he after all. The gremlin knocked the "s" out of "scrapbook," and the whole civilized world of DAR and Ebell reeled. Mrs. Reeve had to be treated for shock at the South Coast Community Hospital, and when the attending physician asked her what had happened, she murmured through ashen lips:

"My 's' is gone. Please find my 's.'"

You can imagine the rest. There's talk the hospital will lose its federal grant and that the State Department of Highways will run its freeway not only through Laguna but right over Mrs. Reeve.

Just let 'em try. Nobody's slapping a woman around in my presence, and especially when it's not her fault. The gremlin did it, a simpering, smirking, sly little imp with a fetish for mischief. You've dragged our Sally into the alley, you've cast a shadow over the rosy hue of People, Places, and Things. You've taken a lovely lady, whose voice is a veritable Peale of lilting laughter and overflowing love for mankind, and you've tarnished her reputation. In the name of Purity, in the name of Honor, for the sake of restoring the one lonely corner in the *Post* where the godly find refuge, I take up the cudgels.

April 18, 1963

Library Week

A few months ago, somebody here in town decided we needed a society known as the Friends of the Library. I had always assumed libraries needed friends about as much as Liz Taylor needed dates, but it turned out I was wrong. As of now, there are only two real Friends of the Library. There's Papa Kroch, who keeps putting new books on the shelves, and there's I (next week is Library Week, and I'm sharpening up those nominative pronouns). I keep taking the books out, to make room for more new ones. This is the natural order of things, of course, a kind of ebb and flow without which the world would go to pot, and anyway I had to make sure nobody was putting books in the library that might be undermining this nation's moral fiber.

Today's Friends of the Library Bookshop, downstairs from the Laguna Beach branch of the Orange County Public Libraries

I mention this because people are always complaining about the library, and I wonder whether they've ever been inside the joint. Oh, you can knock it a bit, I guess. There are those ants on the rear shelves, and some idiot is always scribbling his own comments to himself on the margins of books I've taken out, and you can wait six months on the reserve list for a book you want to read right now. But those are the usual complaints. There's no such thing as a library that is big enough or good enough, and yet when you compare a library with any other repository of man's genius—an art museum, a hall of music, a theater—there is just no contest. You can't go to the movies and see the particular film you want—this week, for instance, I've got a yen for *M.*, or *Monsieur Verdoux,* or *Alexander Nevsky.* I'm stuck with *The Birds*, which, of course, was far superior in its written form. Compared with television's narrow selection, a library—even a small library—is a feast not only for the gourmet but for the gourmand.

Still, as a friendly gesture, and to keep up my current membership, I've got a few suggestions. I approve of phonograph records, and even of some sort of circulation of records, but the word "library" comes from the word *liber*, which means book. (Stick with me and I'll tell you that "book" comes from an Old English word *bóc*, meaning writing tablet.) Every inch of space in a library that is yielded to some other use—however educational or enjoyable—offends this library friend. Throw out the records. The same goes for those glass cases up front where somebody's always putting arrowheads dug out of Lake Onomatopoeia, exciting proof that the pre-Christians were every bit as bloodthirsty as the later models. Libraries are for books, I always say; maybe you can persuade the Starkweathers to install a circulation-record section; if you want to see pre-Columbian arrowheads and other Arty Facts, call Peter Peterman.

He'll show you his collection, and even mix you the best Martini you ever saw, which is more than the librarian will do. It would be nice, too, to chase the Chamber of Commerce out of the next-door building, but then it's always nice to chase out any Chamber of Commerce, and I don't want to confuse the issue here.

The issue is books. You can see 'em at the library all next week. Come to think of it, you can see them the other fifty-one weeks as well. And unlike the fragile doodads you find in museums, there are no Do Not Touch signs on the shelves. Touch them. Take them with you. Make room for more. Keep Papa Kroch busy. Keep me busy. Read yourself awake.

May 23, 1963

When I Grow Up...

My daughter Laurie's third grade class at Aliso, taught by Joan Graham, has again come to the rescue. This time it's a book of ambitions, each kid writing what he wants to do in adulthood. Space does not permit all thirty statements, but even these few reveal the forming of values. You see the conflicts shaping up: the material versus the spiritual; the square versus the odd; the joyously hedonistic versus the soberly productive. The world, in miniature, misspellings and all. Here they are:

"I would like to be a school principal. I would have to learn how to be a principal. Because I have a friend who is a school principal. And so I can give the bad children a spanking."

"When I grow up I will work in a store to get money to buy clothes and some shoes. Then I want to be a lady that tipes in a room with other people that tipes too."

"I'm going to be a fireman. I want to Help people."

"When I grow up I whant to be a trapeze man and do the tripel, and be a show off. I wood be the best of them all! and when they were traning me I wood do better then them, and the job wood be easey."

"When I grow up I'm going to be an explorer. To find out new things. Because I'm curious."

"I want to be a dentist because I wood like to put braces on people."

"I want to be a teacher when I grow up. A teacher's job is to teach children how to spell read print and teach them many other things. I want to be a teacher because I like children and I like to teach things to other people."

"1. I would like to be a football player. 2. You haft to study hard. 3. I want to be a football player because I like football."

"I want to be a teacher because I like children very much. And also I want to be a housewife and have 7 children. And a husband."

"I want to be a secretary because you macke a lot of money. you have to learn to type, and read."

"When I grow up I am going to be a contractor. I thing that my best job would be a contractors, because that my father could help me. You have to know what to do like figure plans and other things."

"When I grow up I want to go to college and learn all about being a school teacher before I get married. When I get married I want to be a housewife. You have to learn to be nice to children not to be strickt. And know most of the answers are. And what you are going to do for the day. I like to handle children!"

"When I grow up I want to be a waitress at a restaurant. I will have to be curtis and get the costermer wants me to get. I want to get a job being a waitress because I think it would be an easy way to make money."

"When I grow up I want to be a docter. I want to take care of people. When I grow up I want to be an artest so I can draw pictures. When I grow up I want to be a lifegard and save people. When I grow up I want to be a pleasman."

"When I Grow Up I want to become a horse trainer. Also I would like to become a girl gambler."

What do you mean, "What are YOU going to do when you grow up?" I'm going to be a realtor, so I can help people. That's what.

May 30, 1963

Muss Universe

Now I've really done it. I've got the Junior Chamber of Commerce on my neck, and when you've got all those aggressive young Big Thinkers on your neck, you'd better reach for a chiropractor or the Flit. Seems I offended the Jaycees by admitting my usual state of perplexity when the Jaycees chose a gal who lives in Downey and works in Anaheim to be Miss Laguna Beach.

Phil Jones, president of the Junior Chamber, has ripped off a three-page bit of philosophy, defending the method of selection. He calls it "the democratic way." Says Jones: "Abraham Lincoln was able to move from his log cabin to the White House. Every girl in America should have an equal chance to become Miss Universe. For example, in Orange County only five girls may go to the Miss California Pageant. (Anaheim, Garden Grove, Huntington Beach, Laguna Beach, and Newport Beach.) It would be quite unfair for girls living in Orange, Tustin, Santa Ana, Capistrano, etc., if they had no chance to compete. But, under the Muss Universe rulings, they may compete for any of the five titles."

Muss Universe, indeed. Actually, I don't think you're thinking big enough. I mean, let's go the whole route. Suppose Pat Young wins? Looking at her, I can't see how she can miss. And then somebody says, in that hot flush of victory, "And where do you live, Pat?" and the kid chokes up and says "Downey."

The next day's papers come out: "Pat Young, a gorgeous 21-year-old from Downey—a suburb of Laguna Beach—has become 1963's Miss Universe. Etc."

How would *you* like it? It's bad we live close to a place called Fountain Valley, but now Downey! That's not all. Then they'll ask: "Where do you work, Pat

Honey?" The kid swallows her pride and stammers: "In Anaheim." I mean, it's no fluke that Jack Benny's been milking laughs out of the word "Anaheim" for over thirty years. Laugh? The whole state—glued to Channel 9—will convulse. Next thing you know the Big Chamber will start advertising Laguna as "The Home of Disneyland." How much can we Lagunans stand? All right, Jones, 'fess up. You're really Mark Engleman in disguise. You're trying to drive people out of town, not lure them in.

I'm sorry, but it won't wash. I mean, it's a bad scene. Let's face facts, Jones. You and the rest of the Baby Chamber are coughing up 300 clams to send a representative to some flesh display, and you've had to fish her out of Downey. It's the worst smack in the eye Laguna's had since the last City Council meeting. Abe Lincoln won't save the day. I mean, under your system, Lincoln never would have lost the senatorial race in 1855, and he'd have been president even sooner. He would just have run in a different state, where Republicans never lose, like Maine or Arizona, instead of Illinois.

And Dick Nixon could live in New York and run for City Council right here in Laguna. After all, didn't Dicky used to come down here on election day to lick his wounds, right on our beach? Think big? You betcha, Baby. All the way. Ted Kennedy made a speech right outside Laguna's City Hall in 1960, and the six or seven people who heard him thought he was pretty funny.

So why not Teddy for the next Jaycee president?

How's this, Honey—"Dear Hedda: I know it's been years since you've lived in Treasure Island, but the Junior Girls' Club seems to need a new president..."

June 13, 1963

Shooting the Breeze

The other evening my wife and I drove through Santa Ana, Tustin, and Orange (we frankly were looking for a bar with folk music, if you want to know), and we were dazzled by the neon display. It was a splendiferous, magnificent, colossal panorama of tasteless advertising, vulgar architecture, and crass commercialism. In short, ugly.

I mention this because last week the Rotary Breeze pre-empted a corner of my page with an editorial blast (you don't know how hard I'm trying not to say "hot air") directed toward more Progress. Progress—with a capital P, and the more capital the better—is a disease known to Rotarians, Chambers of Commerce, and neon manufacturers. It operates under a formula that goes roughly like this: The louder, the better. The brighter, the finer. The uglier, the prettier. It is a formula that equates the words "new commercial enterprise" with culture. It says "beauty" and means skyscraper. The word is spelled Progre$$.

The Rotary Breeze—last week—said Laguna needs a Newporter Inn. It said we need more shops like those in Newport Beach and Corona del Mar. "We need more commercial buildings," the Breeze sighed. We must figure out some way to lure into our narrow downtown streets 100,000 potential shoppers now lurking in the environs. Or we will stagnate.

The stagnation of Laguna Beach began with the first neon bulb and has continued in a majestic, brightly lit downhill march ever since. And the brighter everything is, the less we seem to see. Perhaps that is the trick of it all. Perhaps Progress really means a game of blind-man's bluff, with very loud handkerchiefs over our eyes.

The new Round Table–still the best bar in town—has a bar that isn't even round. And this is the crux. What matters, any more, what we call a thing, provided it is well-lit?

The time has come for a Rotarian and an artist (I'll look until I find one) to stand on opposite sides of a platform before the forum of all Laguna and have it out. Just what is this thing called Progress? Where will it take us? Why do we want 100,000 more shoppers in a town that is overcrowded right now? Why must we look not like Laguna but like Corona del Mar or Newport Beach? Why should we give further study to a marina—as the Breeze suggests? Which is more urgent, a solution to the lack of creative capital or a solution to the lack of creative people? Which is more important, business enterprise or enterprising people?

There is yet a faint hope for the future of Laguna. Not much, but some. The subtle spirit that is Laguna Beach, a marvelous alchemy of worldliness and self-satisfaction and discontent, may yet remain unquenched if we resist now the blandishments of the neon jungle. Happy Harry is calling. Hamburg Haven is yodeling its siren chorus. Rotary Rote is dittoing every other garish corner. The hucksters are selling their (artificially) sweetened syrup. All we have to do is turn our backs. It isn't easy, and the Rotary Breeze will be back in that corner, I'm sure, but let us make up our minds now that we would all be living in Newport Beach if we wanted Laguna Beach to look like Newport Beach, but we live here because there is something here the other guy hasn't yet been able to manufacture.

Debate, anyone?

June 20, 1963

Progress Report on Progress Debate

Talk about Progress, that B.D. is a real swifty. No sooner had I suggested we ought to find out what Progress is before we are stampeded into voting for it than B.D. picked up the challenge.

B.D. says "sophomores are debating about what is Progress," and, by golly, he proves it by debating. Don't feel bad, Big Debater. Kennedy became president that way. There was a difference, of course. Kennedy won his debate.

In the process of coming out five-square for reality, B.D. equates vacant stores with a town's deterioration.

It's a faulty equation. Take that big empty store at the corner of Glenneyre and Forest. When it wasn't empty, it was a commercial enterprise that offered up the frowsiest lettuce I've ever washed out of my teeth. The store represented the biggest supermarket chain in the world, but it forgot one cardinal rule of business an artist understands. You can't sell shoddy. (Yes, "shoddy" is a noun. Look it up.) Is the town better or worse now that the store is empty?

If the purpose of Laguna Beach is to be a better mousetrap (and I'm not sure it is), you've got to decide which mice you're after. Throw up your Newporter-type inns, your shiny new commercial buildings, your marinas with eight hundred parking spaces, and you'll draw somebody into the town, sure, but you'll also drive somebody else out. This is not a threat—heck, you got along without me for years—but simply a reality. If Laguna Beach is to remain to small degree an art colony it must retain a couple of token artists. And the less artistic the town gets—the brighter, bigger, louder, uglier, more commercial, higher-rised, neon-bulbed, build-'em-down-to-the-sands it becomes—the town's charm will diminish.

So the problem remains. Just what is Progress? How do we achieve it? Is it simply birthed by luring in 100,000 shoppers? By attracting new industry? By building a marina? By inviting in tourists and then restricting our beaches? By saying to the artist, "Look here, you deadbeat, you've never met a payroll, so shut up"? By telling the writer, "All you do is make money elsewhere (and spend it here!), so what is your stake in this discussion?"?

As usual, the so-called realists are running around with their heads chopped off. They're for more people and less traffic. They admit there's a problem, but let's not talk about it. Once again the artists are the realists, and the hardheaded realists are living a fantasy. Come down here, Big Debater, where we can talk. Let us stop playing blindman's bluff. What are our goals? Where do we start? What do you mean by Progress?

Moe Nark?

I suppose it's a form of my intellectual snobbism or some other social disease, but I am stricken by the sign at the corner of Thalia and the Coast Highway, advertising yet another housing development here in Laguna. Ah, Progress!

It's called Monarc Estates. Yep, Monarc. They've knocked the "h" out of Monarch, which is, I suppose, real democratic, but now I can't pronounce it. Is it Moe Narse? Moe Nark? Monn Arc? Still, bad as this is, the crusher on the sign is the use of the possessive pronoun "its" spelled with an apostrophe. I'm probably unfair for assuming a man who can't spell his own name and doesn't know a pronoun from a subject-verb contraction isn't likely to build a solid house, but I'll pass, thank you.

Not that the Monarc sign is as garish an eyesore as the one on Glenneyre, touting a new co-op called Seaview Terrace. I haven't been able to check the sign for typographical errors, but that's because I have to blink every time I drive by. Thus far, I've counted five colors on the fairly small board—red, green, yellow, black, and white—and if some Big Dealer tells me black is no color, I'll give him a colorless eye. All the sign needs is a neon light and the American flag and you'll think you're playing pinball.

No, Honey, I am not knocking the American flag. You're just getting sensitive.

July 18, 1963

Bluff Called

Claire Gregan has questioned my use of "blindman's bluff," instead of "blindman's buff." I'd have blamed the usual back-room gremlin, except my mother taught me never to lie, especially when there's evidence against you. They've got my copy back there, with "bluff" as big as life, and I plead guilty. It's not the first time I've tried to bluff my way through. I know it's buff, but on occasion I look down my nose and, fighting vertigo every inch of the way, I decide t' hell with what's correct and cater to the base tastes of my public. Along comes a Claire Gregan every time to call me.

You're right, Claire, and I apologize. It's blindman's buff. You know, put on the scarf, spin him around, and let him loose, trying to buffet (not bluffet) anybody in his way.

The thing I'm afraid of now is that by my confession I'll lose face. No longer will my faithful few read the col'm and say, "Well, old Woody's been done in again by a typesetter." For instance, a few issues back I said "furp" was an intransitive verb, and it came out "intramsitive." I can see the sneers on the lips of Gregan and Wainwright and the other reader. "Intramsitive, indeed. Thinks it's a riding-around kind of word. No wonder they bury him in that corner." And when I go up to Big Donor next Christmas, hat in hand, asking for another raise, B.D.'ll say: "What for? To badger the language some more? Go read your dirty dictionary."

It's a lesson. You talk about Progress, you battle the marina mob and the garish-sign boys, you stand on the lonely ramparts holding back the tide and other mixed metaphors, and all they can say is: "C'mon Woody, shape up. Knock the 'ell out of 'bluff.'"

Speaking of trams, as I think we were, that gay old open tram whizzing tourists through our streets has the darnedest sign. It says on the back: "10¢ Per. Ride." It's the period after "Per" that gets me. What's "Per." short for? Person? Perfect? Perspicacious? Persnickety? I'll promise to say "buff" if you guys erase that period.

And while I'm word-happy, I've been thumbing my way through our little blue directory, just reading the names. As somebody once said: Lousy plot, but what a cast of characters!

The caretaker at the funeral home is Amen; the Good Humor man's name is Leak; we've got a barber named Peck; and a guy named Gill owns a liquor store. There's a maintenance man named Handy; a student named Creed; a salesman named Goforth; our lifeguard captain is Rod Riehl. An engineer for the phone company is named Heard. We've got a Husk, a Hull, and a Corn; we've got a Yolk, a White, a Cocke, and a couple of Eggers. There's a Macbeth and a Hamlet; we've got a Lent and a Borrow. A man named Glass is a jeweler. There's an auto salesman named Lemon; man named Lees works for a firm named Seaboard; we've even got a guy named Male. It's a lively town—we've got an Ogle, a Bottom, a Quirk, a Champagne, and a Lawless. You've got to keep your eyes open. We've got a Swindell, a Trapp, a Slicker, and a Trickey. But mainly it's a balanced town: We've got a Low and a Haigh; a Hair and a Wiggs; a Small and a Bigg; a Gunn and a Dove; an Urban and a Hicks; a Hill and a Vail; a Younghusband and a Batchelor; we've got Fogg and Sun. There's even a marine named Loveless, and another marine named Loving.

If ever you're worried about Laguna, have faith. We've got Verity and Heartz and Good and Will. And don't forget Piety.

August 29, 1963

Butterfly

The first time I heard bits of *Madame Butterfly* I was five or six years old. We owned an old hand-cranked Victrola and a scratchy record of Puccini arias, and my mother used to sit with me and tell me the whole maudlin story of Butterfly and how she was done in. (My mother had her problems, too.) Then she and I used to weep over the music.

I am a sucker for *Madame Butterfly*, and I'll be there this weekend, weeping for her. It is, to me, the most lovely, the most romantic, the most lyric, and the most pathetic of all operas, and though I know you're supposed to like *Götterdammerung* and *Otello* and *Don Giovanni* better, give me *Butterfly* and a bucket for my tears every time.

Not that it isn't a dramatically good work. It is one of the finest ever written, its essential story quality too often lost in the lyric sentimentality that abounds. *Butterfly* is an ethnically, historically, psychologically valid drama. Historically, it represents what happened to the Orient after the Open Door was thrust upon it. Ethnically, it represents the smug white man, dallying with a woman of another and lesser race, using her, and then discarding her. Psychologically, it represents that lasting stain of guilt which is the true white man's burden and which forces the master race back to the scene of his crime and back to his victim, for the therapy of forgiveness. It has other and almost total psychological validity in its portrayal of the sweet patience of the victim who longs to be victimized. And, of course, it has that added, unwitting monstrous irony today, in that the action takes place in Nagasaki! We keep going back to the scenes of our crime, we keep needing forgiveness, and we keep blotting out our crime with further crime.

Butterfly has a libretto that fairly glitters with dramatic subtleties, and in English they will surely be more appreciated, even if the lyrics lose some of their purity of sound. For instance, in the opening scene—after the U.S. consul warns Pinkerton not to tear those dainty wings of Butterfly by ill use of her love—Pinkerton retorts airily that no harm can come from a mutually enjoyed passion, and then he says: "Whisky?" and both men forget Butterfly to indulge in another drink. You know, then and there, that Butterfly's wings are not only going to be torn, they're going to be torn off, and you further know that the voice of the American conscience and the American government, the consul, is tinged with its own hypocrisy in its dealing with other peoples. Seconds later, Butterfly's exquisite far-off voice is heard, and the first words she sings are (according to my translation): "There's one more step to climb."

What a step it turns out to be!

The opera season—thus far—has been a marvelously artistic success, but for the same reason that makes Jerry Lewis and Ma and Pa Kettle popular but somehow puts opera companies in the red, it has not been a financial success. The Festival of Opera can use more angels–they've found a host of them already—and if you can't make it to the Irvine Bowl, or even if you can, perhaps you can reach into your jeans and send a check to the Festival of Opera, 650 Broadway. Butterfly will die these next three nights, and it will be a glorious death and one to weep over, but opera must not be allowed to die in

Laguna. Not after two such beautiful seasons. Because a death like that will not be glorious but tragic and needless. All it takes to keep opera alive and thriving in Laguna is money, plus a love for this most beautiful of art forms.

September 5, 1963

Timber!

It's the end of the tourist season, and man should love
his neighbor even if he's from Nebraska, but the fact is,
I can't remember a period when a Lagunan could pick a
fight with such ease.

Want to tear down the telephone poles in town?
There's a battle shaping up in the City Council, now
that Councilman Dick Sears has suggested that all new
tracts put their telephone wires underground. Sears
says, and means, the telephone wires at any future development, but once the Culture Cabal hears about this,
they'll be for uprooting every old power pole in town,
singing "T' hell with JJay's flowers" as they rip away.

Can't really blame them either. The real eyesore in
Laguna is not the midway we call the Coast Highway,
although that is a garish, gaudy monstrosity; it is not the
"For Rent" signs that sit in cobwebbed corners of deserted downtown stores, although they are grayly forlorn
and depressing; it is not the squared-off scale model
of a marina, although that is a desecration; it is not the
brown bulldozed scars that now pock Top of the World
and Bluebird Canyon, although they are sad, cruel,
and ugly beyond words. The real eyesore in this (still)
lovely town is the tangle of black wire that cuts across
every inch of view. If I turn my head—this minute—to
the left, as I sit at my desk, this is what I see: the leaves
of my sycamore tree, a lovely red-tile white Spanish
house across the street, a roof of red bougainvillea, the
leaves of my acacia tree, and fifteen rows of power lines.
Fifteen rows! My sycamore tree is perpetually stunted
and scarred; every few months the utility people come
around and gently ask permission to amputate more
branches, so that the tree does not encroach upon the

wires. The living is cut down to support the dead. This asking permission is a bit of empty etiquette. I have no choice. If I refuse, there is a good chance the power would go dead on our block, and who am I to discommode my neighbors (and my wife)? So my sycamore is a thick-leaved dwarf.

It is a good fight Dick Sears has picked, but as I say, it is not the only fight in town. I see by the papers (as some radio comedian used to sing thirty-plus years back; I'll give—free—the original manuscript of this column to the first reader who can tell me the name of the comedian) nobody has protested the building of a three-acre shopping center at Top of the World. Ah, Progress! Remember when Top of the World was old and woodsy, and you could drive leisurely around the circle at the peak and see the canyons and the ocean and then drive back down uncluttered roads and green hills? Pretty soon we'll be able to zip up the hill to buy something. But what we'll have lost we'll never be able to buy again.

You don't like these fights? You can fight the LOCCA fight against the proposed bisecting Freeway; you can fight (for or against) the beach bond; you can get right into that dandy free-for-all election to the Festival of Arts board of directors—nine candidates running for three seats. Wanna fight? There's no need to run off to Washington, D.C., to demonstrate, or to Birmingham, to take on Bull Connors and the rest of the police dogs down there. You can stay right here in sleepy, sun-drenched Laguna, at the conclusion of our money-lovin' tourist season, and find a swell fight on every corner.

No, Honey, the question isn't whether Bull Connors will sue; I'm only worried that I've insulted the dogs.

September 26, 1963

Bill Bored

The sight of two new billboards on Laguna Canyon
Road is the most disturbing recent manifestation of the
commercial world that keeps encroaching on us. I have
no idea what will go on the billboards—they are blank,
as I write this—but whatever, it will be ugly, another
ugly attempt to bludgeon us to buy or live or vote in a
certain way. I don't like it. And I think something should
be done about it. Either now, before they paint the
words and pictures on the billboards, or soon, before the
next board goes up. I know that billboards are on county
soil, not city, and it is therefore up to the county government to determine whether anything of a prohibitory
nature may be done, and I also know from eight years of
living here that Orange County government is famous
for its laissez-faire attitude, which really means, "Stop
bothering us; we have to sleep, too."

Well, it may be county land, but it is part of the resi-
dential area of Laguna Beach, and it is our most direct
link to the inland world, where ahead lie Los Angeles
and Fullerton and other hick towns. Sometimes we
have to go to L.A. or to Fullerton, and—even faster—we
have to get back. We drive the canyon road. And those
billboards are over our heads as we drive, not over the
county supervisors' heads. It is we who must live with
the billboards. It is we who will be bombarded by the
pictures, assailed by the lettered blandishments. So the
law may not see Laguna's right to make a noise about
the billboards, but common sense and a sort of squat-
ters' sovereignty surely deserve a hearing. There are
10,000 people in Laguna Beach, and I'll bet Alton Allen
or whoever represents this piece of county road that
nearly as many of those 10,000 people would be against
turning the canyon road into an advertisers' avenue

as would be against a coastal freeway. We are against both, for the same reason. Not because they infringe on property rights or in some way depress property values. Those are the cries of the property-minded who are gradually becoming as mechanized, as automated, as dehumanized as the billboard faces. We are against the billboards and a bisecting Freeway because they are affronts to the eye, to the soul, to the aesthetics that are just as much part of man as is his house or his barbershop or his Honda. The billboards shock me; they interrupt my pleasure; they uproot nature; they substitute for nature; they obstruct my vision, and I do not mean merely my physical vision.

There is another reason I hate these billboards. Their height offends me. I discovered this when I asked myself whether I am against all signs in all places. The answer is No. I do not mind, and I even feel at home with, Cather's Kilns, Clover's Candles, Mrs. Smith's inn for cats, all of which are advertising signs on the canyon road. But they are all eye-level, and it makes an enormous difference. We meet on even terms, Mrs. Cather and I. But the billboards loom over my head, they assume a superiority, they oppress me.

Mainly, however, they bore me. Don't the advertisers know how bored we are with their continual shrieking, their harassing of us? Don't they know we demand surcease from their orders? There is a freshness to the canyon; each time I drive I see a new color, a new rock formation, a more leisurely cow, a handsomer horse. I am relaxed, and I am invigorated by this ten-mile stretch of silent nature. But plaster the stretch with more screams that we buy Pepsodent or Cortese or Man Tan and I guarantee you that ten or twenty or fifty Lagunans will make a note in their heads to buy instead the unseen, unheard competitor.

Honey, keep your eye on the road. Don't let those damn cows distract you.

October 17, 1963

Negro Haircuts

Two weeks ago a Negro boy who resides in Laguna and attends Orange Coast College walked into a barbershop in the downtown area and was told by a barber: "I don't know how to cut your hair." The boy walked out.

Several weeks before, a Negro walked into another shop and was told—in more or less the same language —that the barber did not know how to cut his hair.

There is not a court in the state that will tolerate this shallow pretext, and it is only the patience and tolerance of Negroes in this town that have kept these barbers and others from being hauled before the law.

It is such a tawdry excuse, this refusal to cut Negroes' hair because it is somehow different. If the argument is—as it sometimes goes—"We can't cut kinky, curly hair like that," I'll bring in white men with kinky, curly hair like that, and there isn't a barber in town who'll turn them away. And even if the barber honestly feels he can't cut kinky, curly hair like that, there are Negroes who are willing to have the barber learn on them. They'll sit there and pay for the teaching, too.

Other barbers, on occasion, will admit another reason for their refusal to serve Negroes. Two barbers have told me: "If I cut their hair, I'll lose my white customers."

For one thing, I doubt it. For two, where will the white customers go if *all* the barbers in town decide the time has come to stop this form of discrimination? And for three, though I sympathize with any man who loses a fraction of his business, there is no question where my greater sympathies lie. They lie with the human being who wants to be treated no differently from any other human being.

There is one hope, other than dragging the barbers into court. It is that the barbers will see reason. The morality of the issue is against them, history is against them, and, what is probably more pertinent to their pocketbook, the law is against them. Perhaps they *will* lose some business if they start cutting Negroes' hair; they'll surely lose money if they don't. There are Negroes in Laguna who have finally decided: Now. They don't want to run on up to Santa Ana, Long Beach, and even Los Angeles for a haircut. They want their hair cut right here in town. Now. They demand it, as their right. And so does the state of California demand it for them. Listen:

"All citizens within the jurisdiction of this State are entitled to the full and equal accommodations, advantages, facilities, and privileges of inns, restaurants, hotels, eating houses, places where ice cream, soft drinks of any kind are sold for consumption on the premises, barber shops, bath houses, theaters, skating rinks, public conveyances, and all other places of public accommodation or amusement, subject only to conditions of limitations established by law and applicable alike to all citizens."

This is California's public-accommodations law, passed back in 1905. In 1959 the law was made more potent, to cover all people "in all business establishments of every kind whatsoever."

This is the law. For every violation, the violator must pay actual damages, plus $250. Two hundred and fifty dollars is a hundred twenty-five haircuts.

Frankly, I cannot believe the barbers in this town are not law-abiding. Perhaps they never knew the law existed. I also cannot believe they are unreasonable men. I cannot believe they would deliberately choose to throw away their hard-earned money to continue this shabby insult.

October 24, 1963

Costa Nostra

I was wrong. The marina mob hadn't blown town after all. They've just been lying low, waiting for the recent rash of out-of-town marina disasters to ease themselves from our memory. Nobody's talking much about the mess at Marina Del Rey these days. The wrecked pilings, the swamped boats, the submerged moorings, the washed-out homes, the sand slopped over the highway—all have come and gone, and the marina mob has kept its weather-eye peeled, its finger on our pulse, and has decided the time is now. It's got to be now, because who knows when the next marina, elsewhere, will go under?

Now they've got a multimillion-dollar bond issue, which won't—naturally!—cost anybody anything, and they've got some statements from handpicked engineers that a marina at the foot of Heisler Park is feasible. Whaddya know!

Unfortunately, the marina boys don't know when to quit. Show us the plans, trot out the engineers, and then keep quiet. But, no, they've got to ramble on. This time it's Ray Miller, one of the marina leaders, warning us: "If you don't vote for this marina, the state may come in and do as it pleases with the land." (You call it blackmail; I'll just call it friendly persuasion.) Now we have the threat of state control hanging over our heads. Now we have the old demon, creeping socialism, to contend with. Well, it's Halloween time, and we know a hobgoblin when we see one.

But even that isn't all. Miller goes on. He tells us his marina will provide 2,000 feet of sandy beach, and he thinks we will all fall down dead with the wonder of it. Miller explains why his 2,000 feet of sandy beach will be such an improvement. "After all, there's only rocks out there now."

Only rocks out there! You can see it, can't you? The Arizona chamber of commerce rushing over to the Grand Canyon and saying: "It's only a big hole. Fill her in." Or the Massachusetts Improvement Association saying: "That big rock in the water. It's in the way. Rip it out."

Activists in Laguna Beach successfully fought off a marina, thereby preserving "one of the most breathtaking sights man's eye can light upon."

Is all this necessary? Must it be spelled out for Miller and his marina band? Do they have to be told that a rock in the ocean, where the waves hit and foam over, can be—and often is—one of the most breathtaking sights man's eye can light upon? I'm not much for seascape paintings, but there's no disputing the lore of rock and sea, the hold it has on man's soul, his aesthetic nature. And I'm not much for remembering church hymns, but as I recall it (and you can correct me), it goes: "Just like the rock, standing by the water, we shall not be moved."

So you can, if you wish, bring about this bond issue, where the people will vote whether they want a marina or not. You can waste your time and mine, your money and mine, and put it on a ballot. But it's a lost cause, and I am dumbfounded at the tenacity of these people who insist on destroying, who insist on replacing beauty with ugliness, and who keep insisting that nature be re-drawn in man's image instead of the other way around.

November 21, 1963

Double-faced

I have before me a carbon of a letter from the Orange
Planning Commission director, relating to the billboards
put up by Ross Cortese along Laguna Canyon Road.
The second paragraph—and the meat of the letter—
goes:

"These directional signs, located on the developer's
property, were permitted for a period not to exceed five
years by the Orange County Planning Commission on
June 12, 1963. The signs are double-faced, 44 feet by 10
feet, with a minimum 10-foot ground clearance. One of
the signs is in a commercially zoned area, the other is
located on property zoned for a cemetery. These are the
only signs permitted by this variance to be located on
Laguna Canyon Road."

Whenever I see the word "variance" my hackles
rise. Does this mean it was necessary for Cortese to get
the county planners—those far-sighted visionaries!—to
permit Cortese to do something a zoning or sign ordinance ordinarily forbids? Does it mean the county
planners actually went out of their way to accede to this
garish monstrosity?

We have five years to live with these signs. Some
of us have less, of course. The canyon road has always
been a graveyard of twisted steel and flesh, and the
irony of the phrase "zoned for a cemetery" is ghoulish
indeed. I drove the canyon road the other evening, and
not only do Cortese's signs offend by day, they appear
to imperil by night. Coming into Laguna, you see the
sign that is farthest from our city limits, and at night
what you see is 440 square feet of a glaring white sur-
face that causes the motorist—or at least this motorist—

to jerk the head away from the road so as to clear the vision. But the second sign—the one that faces Laguna at the intersection with the road leading to El Toro—is far worse. Coming into town, you see a string of bright white bulbs. I counted six—four of them extremely glaring, two of them muted, perhaps by the angle at which they are placed. They hit you like so many white bullets—a pair of bright lights, a pair of muted lights, a pair of bright lights—and my first thought was: There are three cars off there someplace; I could imagine three sets of headlights. It's more than confusing; it is downright deadly, and the cemetery is surely the proper place for it.

I don't know what we can do; we surely can see the billboards are not renewed in five years. But can't we do something now? Can't we put out the lights at night? The billboards are up in all their flaunting ugliness; they are huge impediments on the canyon floor by day. But must we see them at night, other than as dark lurking shadows? Can't we have the nights? Cortese has the days. Isn't it enough? Will a perceptive traffic officer— or somebody—drive out there and confirm the peril Cortese has created, and, if for no other reason than safety, can't he darken those double-faced signs?

Utterly Utt

While we're going around dimming things, can't anybody persuade Jimmy Utt to keep his mouth shut? First it was a proposed amendment to the Constitution to make this nation a Christian nation—all of us, Christians and Jews and Moslems and non-believers—by simple fiat. Then came his blast that Jessica Mitford's book exposing the exorbitant cost of funerals was some sort of communistic plot. Now it's the revelation that an Utt

91

newsletter created an ugly rumor to the effect that a military exercise in Georgia was part of a plot by the U.N. to take over America. Apparently 50,000—at least—believed the rumor, according to mail received by Senator Tom Kuchel. It was wild and woolly improvisation on Utt's part; it was also wildly inaccurate. Don't take my word for it, of course. Take Utt's. He got on the air the other night and admitted he'd been wrong. Wasn't that manly of him?

2

Hello There!! by Woody Cove

Village Sun, 1971

October 1–14, 1971

I never would have thought I'd give up my long faithful
love, but I think I've found a replacement. As much as
I slaver over Baskin-Robbins's Jamoca Almond Fudge, I
have to confess Carvel's Chocolate Swiss Almond Fudge
is even better. In case you don't know, Carvel is that
new ice-cream joint at the north end of town, where
Emerald Bay residents sneak out and climb over the
wall when the guards aren't looking to see how the free
world lives. The real advantage Carvel has over B-R's
31 flavors is that nobody has discovered it as yet, so you
don't have to wait an hour for a two-scoop cone.

This town has suddenly turned into a gourmet
paradise. And cheap, too. If there are better sandwiches
in the world (and for 89 cents) than at Stottlemyer's, I
haven't found them. My favorite? A Marlon Brando.
Try it. This business of using real names for sandwiches
is fun. I've got a few local suggestions. How's about a
Tommie Gunn sandwich: the police chief on the griddle.
A Dick Toomey sandwich: you don't eat it, you drink it.
A Loren Haneline sandwich: it varies from day to day.
Ed Lorr: dog meat, between two strips of bark. Birch
bark, of course. And a Vernon Spitaleri sandwich: 10
cents worth of baloney. A Woody Cove? Tongue on wry,
of course.

While we are examining my exquisite taste in all matters, let me tell you about Mission Bank, soon to set up quarters, and halves and dollars, on the corner of Glenneyre and St. Ann's. This will be our first friendly neighborhood bank, the only such institution off the downtown drag. The bank is a dandy idea; people will be able to walk over and give up all their money without climbing into their cars and poisoning the rest of us. Unfortunately, Mission Bank isn't satisfied simply to have a handsome bank and a local monopoly. As a sign says on the construction fence, it has free goodies in store for you. One of the free goodies is a monstrous pole sign, 25 feet high, 75 square feet on each face. Naturally it's a two-faced sign. Which makes it over twice as big as the Tic Toc atrocity; it makes it, in fact, as large as any pole sign in Laguna Beach and much bigger than anything yet on Glenneyre. It's big, all right, but is it ugly! It doesn't just say "Mission Bank" and let it go at that. There's an ersatz bell and an arch and a wrought-iron gate that leads to nowhere. It is a sign for the neighborhood, provided the neighborhood is in Mission Viejo.

The sign isn't needed. There's plenty of room for a wall sign that would do the job nicely. It isn't likely people aren't going to know the bank is there: Mission has spent a million dollars in the building and land. You can't miss it. Just look for the place where those two gorgeous old palm trees used to be.

So why a gigantic pole sign? No reason, except to catch the eye of the person driving by and imprint "Mission Bank" on his consciousness. Sort of like a billboard.

We ripped down the billboards in the Canyon and elsewhere in Laguna. The time would appear ripe for a moratorium on pole signs. Or else be willing to turn Glenneyre into the same sort of neon jungle that has taken root on Coast Highway. I am telling you all this because the Board of Zoning Adjustment turned down Mission Bank's pole sign, and now there's talk of an appeal to the City Council. On a quiet Wednesday night, when everybody is drowsing, you might just see or hear Ed Lorr or Pete Ostrander or the Mayor, still caught up in the nonsense that Bigger is Better, come on strong for poor old Mission Bank and its rejected erection.

As a matter of fact, you can bank on it.

October 15–21, 1971

Honored?

You better believe it.

By the time you read this, if you read, I will have been honored as the Unitarian Big Mouth of the Year at a dinner I won't even have to pay for. The Big Woman freeloads with me. This annual dinner is an old and honorable tradition among the Unitarians here in Laguna–it's been going on since last year. I don't know what one is supposed to do to deserve such an honor, but maybe it's because I eat more cookies at Unitarian affairs (yes, Virginia, Unitarians have affairs—it's only Episcopalians who don't have affairs) than any other male present. Of course, there's never any other male present, which is another reason I show up. All those ladies. So I am their speaker of the year. Kinda makes those stale cookies worthwhile.

After that, later this month, I'm to speak at UCI's Friends of the Library annual dinner. The Big Woman asked me, "How do they select the annual speaker?" and I said, "At random."

But enough about me. It's the Friends' affair that is so intriguing. It begins with a champagne social hour at seven, which like all hours since the invention of Freud lasts only 50 minutes, at which time we stagger in and have dinner. During dinner, guess what happens? They show movies! Yep. They're showing what they call a "short light film" that's supposed to provide the comic relief either to the dinner or to me, I can't tell which.

Think of it. The TV dinner has now become institutionalized. You watch something to keep your mind off the canned peas, or you eat the canned peas so you won't truly mind what's on the screen. Then after the dinner and the movie, they get me. Sort of from soup to nut.

Actually, I'm used to this sort of thing. I get honored all the time. One year the phone rang and it was the president of the alumni association of my old college, congratulating me because they'd just named me Alumnus of the Year. Naturally I said, "How come? Weren't there any doctors in the audience?" The alumni bigwig (actually he's bald, but we call people like that bigwigs; it's an old bit of slang, real heavy back in the 1930s) sort of chuckled and said, "It's not that. We really want you. You are our Alumnus of the Year," or some such flattery.

So I said, "Thank you. What happens now?" and he said, "You appear at our annual dinner—all very formal—and we give a plaque and you make a speech." He probably said, "You deliver an address," but that's the way bigwigs talk. Real hairy. And I said, "How do I get to the dinner? It's 3,000 miles away. Who pays the airfare?" The bigwig suddenly stopped chuckling and he said, "Well, of course, hmm, well, hmph, you do." And I said, "For $300 I get a plaque?" and he said, "If you want to put it that way," and I said, "I'll tell you what. Why don't you just mail me the plaque?" and he said, "No soap." (That's another old bit of slang. He didn't really mean no soap. We all washed in those days, carrying water on our backs for miles to the old zinc tub in the kitchen every Saturday night.) He said, "If you won't appear to deliver the address, you can't be our Alumnus of the Year," and I said, "Well, it was nice being Alumnus of the Year for three minutes anyway," and that's how Murray Schisgal became Alumnus of the Year at my old college instead. He happened to be in New York, so he didn't have to spend $300 for the plaque. Naturally the dinner is free.

Now you know that Woody Cove isn't just any sort of slob. He's a very particular sort of slob. He accepts your free dinners provided they're free. Friends of the Library won't even have to pay my gas. With champagne, movies, and canned peas, I make my own. Come to think of it, that's 19 miles each way, 38 miles total, and at the usual 10 cents per mile you can charge for such things on your income tax, I'll be out $3.80. Maybe while they're watching the movie I'll steal the silverware.

3

The Village Character

Laguna Beach Independent, 2003–2004

January 17, 2003

I stood on the floor of the law library in the University of Coimbra in central Portugal. Coimbra (pronounced Kweem-bra) was once the capital of Portugal, a city on a hill with a river snaking below and a magnificent university which tourists are invited to visit. I visited, and fell in love.

The university was established in 1290—take that, Harvard, you callow youth—and its law library began stocking books printed by one of Europe's oldest commercial printing presses beginning in 1520.

As I stood, a sliver of sunlight pierced the gallery above where books stood on neat shelves. The soft vellum bindings glowed like liquid gold. A ladder leaned against a shelf for a librarian to climb and seek out a book for a requesting researcher. This is a functioning library—faculty and special students are permitted to hold these books in their hands.

And the books are among the oldest printed in the world!

I am an easy mark when it comes to books. To me there is no such thing as an ugly book. I even own the hate-filled polemic *The Elders of Zion*, edited by that anti-Semite Henry Ford.

So this was overwhelming, golden-spined books off a hot press nearly five hundred years earlier. I fought off tears.

A month later back in Laguna, I learned another library story. This one chilled my blood.

Our city library is part of the Orange County system. Its budget is determined by the Board of Supervisors and its bean counters. The total books' acquisition budget for our library, fiscal year 2001/2002, had been $69,364. For this year it has been cut to $21,628, a slash of 70%. Look at it this way: if our library had received a hundred new books last year, it will receive thirty books this year.

Yes, I know. Cops and firefighters are what's needed. Books are frills.

Not to me, not to me. Books sustain me. Cops and firefighters, bless 'em, save our lives today. Books save our lives forever. We need them all.

It is not just that books are viewed as unimportant. It is a pandemic disease, this indifference to history. Scrap the old, ring in the new. We see it in the first City Council meetings, a contempt for what happened earlier. The Village Entrance is not a project, one councilmember tells us, it is just a design. Well, it's a design for a project. Why else did we pay to sponsor a contest in which some of the best architectural firms around strutted their stuff? It was to determine what our village entrance would look like.

But not now. After all, that was the old council. This is the new. (New as in Elizabeth Pearson: all the rest of you look like the same old faces.)

To some of these folk, history goes back as far as last Thursday. Retire the winning design. And while you're at it, put it on the same back shelf as the Vision process.

After all, the Vision process took two thousand Lagunans three years to finalize. Three years! That's ancient history.

And books! Who needs 'em? Books are for Portuguese law students. Books and history—they're so—so retro, so yesterday.

Damn right!

January 30, 2003

I cannot recall so many god-awful developments threatening Laguna at the same time. How do I hate them? Let me count the ways.

1. *The Artists' Walk.* This one has no relationship to the Laguna we know and love. The property owner calls it Artists' Walk, but he thinks Disney Drive. Or Drivel. It is an eyesore. The property abuts Art-A-Fair and the city employee parking lot at the nexus of the proposed Village Entrance and the arts district. It would provide 19,000 square feet of retail space and nineteen artists' live/work units. The live/work units are a worthy idea, except the units are 1,500 square feet each, the size of modest houses but not artists' studios unless the artist is Wyland, who needs all that space for his live whale models. The property owner also envisions two restaurants, one right next to Tivoli Two. Doesn't he have the good sense to look around at what's there? What's there is Laguna Beach, not Anaheim. He also suggests an upscale men's clothing store. Can't you see all those artists walking around in Armani and Bill Blass? I'd rather see another T-shirt shop.

2. *Driftwood Estates.* This one will define our current City Council. The council seems to salivate over Driftwood. One councilmember asks the city attorney if the project conforms to the General Plan. If it does, one may infer, he will love it. Forget conformity, I say—think safety, health, and well-being.

It's not safe, healthy, or conducive to well-being. It is conducive to fear and loathing. It is a fire waiting to ignite. It has one ingress and egress on a road as wide as a number 2 pencil. Even at seven units it's too dense. At fifteen units it's a blood clot in your carotid. And why fifteen units? Because somebody at some time in the past took the natural watercourse and corked it, turned it into an unnatural watercourse and wiped it off the map. Now we have room for fifteen units. No we don't. We have gridlock. Imagine a fire engine laboring up that steep hill and fifteen families fleeing down the same hill in their cars.

What this project is is a bribe. Here, the developer says, take 218 unbuildable acres as a gift to the City's open space, and give us in turn fifteen houses at a million dollars per house (I'm being conservative), and we'll call it a deal. What a deal!

3. *The Dip House.* That's where it will be located, in the dip on Glenneyre between Calliope and Bluebird Canyon Drive, where the village turns rustic, where the shops on Glenneyre vanish. A creek wends its way beneath the pending house—unless, of course, someone corks this one as well. Park your car and walk to the building stakes on the uphill side of Glenneyre and look through to what you won't be able to see once the house is built. The loss is heartbreaking.

How does this happen? The council doesn't understand its role. A few years ago a councilmember elected with Treasure Island development money blurted out at a council meeting, "We're in partnership with the Athens Group on Treasure Island." Right? Dead wrong. The only partnership the council has is with the people it represents. That's us. It is not the council's role to make sure a dreadful project conforms to the General Plan. It is not its role to permit a subdivision that goes against every grain of Laguna Beach. It is the council's role to make sure fire engines can get through to fires. I know, I know. I am whistling in a graveyard. The votes will pile up, 4–1 for this desecration, 4–1 for that monstrosity. Armani suits in a denim village. A lovely canyon blocked from view. The future is drear with this council and its apparent mind-set.

Still, have courage. We lived through high-rise threats and a long-gone councilmember trapping cats. Spring is just around the corner. And the baseball season is two months away!

April 11, 2003

The Dip House—Take Two

The first time I ever saw a fox outside a zoo was on
Glenneyre Street. It was a small adult who slipped my
surveillance and ducked into the brush by the side of
the road and then down into the canyon.

We're talking about the proposed dip house on
Glenneyre between Bluebird Canyon and Calliope.
I have no idea whether my fox still lives there. Some
fox apparently does. I am indebted to Jim Sieg, an old
hand in the neighborhood, for a list of animals sighted
recently, plus the birds who hang out there, and the
indigenous plants.

I was thrilled to see "gray fox" listed at number two;
the whole list follows: Mule deer, gray fox, coyote, rac-
coon, skunk, cottontail, opossum, frogs, butterflies. The
birds include hawks and owls, hummingbirds and jays,
warblers and sparrows, a Western tanager, an Oregon
junco, and a red-breasted nuthatch, plus a dozen or so
more. The indigenous plants are the lemonade berry,
Catalina cherry, Torrey pine, live oak, nopal, Mexican
ash, agave, willow, and perhaps coastal sage. This last
has a question mark.

It won't shame Yellowstone Park. It is a mere 3,000-
plus square feet of greenery, a taste of the wild smack
in the middle of the village. It must be protected. And
the city is falling down on its job. So it will be up to the
residents to fight this battle.

At 1530 Glenneyre architect/owner Jeff Garner
wishes to build a small house, right on the town's only
perennial river; it runs all year, sometimes a trickle,
other times a torrent. During the March rains the entire
lot was covered by a foot or more of water. The architect wants to build a house where no house ought to

be built. It's as simple as that, and the city is making it easier for him.

The great David Brower, he of Sierra Club and Friends of the Earth fame, once described the fight between a developer and a preservationist as a coin toss. "Heads, the developer wins," he said. "Tails—well, we'll have to flip again."

In a matter like this the city is asked by the developer to issue a negative declaration—a document that says the project will have no significant impact on the environment. If the developer receives such a report, he doesn't have to file an environmental impact report.

The city, in its infinite wisdom, has made such a finding. It has filed a negative declaration, a nineteen-page document that lists all the possible impacts. Nearly all are dismissed out of hand.

The first area it tackles is that of aesthetics. No significant impact. What in the world were they thinking? All you have to do is stand at the project and look through the story poles. What you see now will not be seen once the house is built. It will be lost. The house will wipe out the entrance to the canyon. It will obliterate what is now a lovely view of the canyon. Here today, gone tomorrow.

The document proceeds: Will building the house in front of the trees, the bushes, the animal habitats, the town's only running perennial river—will the house substantially degrade these scenic resources? No. Will this house substantially degrade the existing visual character? No. Does it degrade its surroundings? No.

It is a document of madness. It turns the mundane world upside down. What's right is wrong. What's beautiful is worthless. What's impactful doesn't hurt.

Have faith. The Design Review Board will probably not buy into this appalling hustle. Members will look at the variances and turn them down. They will deny the project. Whoopee! We've won! Stop dreaming. It's just beginning. The architect will appeal to the City Council, famous for giving developers what they want. So the denial by the DRB will be overturned, and the council may say to the developer, "Do what you want, my son. Pillage away. It's all yours."

But you don't know that any of this will happen. Keep fighting. Go to City Hall and read this infamous negative declaration. Then you must write your comments. You have until April 30 to get your comments in the file. But I wouldn't wait until April 30—the meeting on the dip house is May 1, at 6 p.m. Be there to talk about the project and why it makes you sick. Celebrate May Day at City Hall. Do it by beating back the application. Save this piece of land and our river. Think of the possible loss of the site. The site is the creature of sixty or seventy millennia, a masterwork by rivers and rain, etching Bluebird Canyon. What we see at this particular site is the wellspring of Bluebird Canyon. What you want is to save it, with the bloom of creation still on it.

So be there, and speak up. And when we all do, is it over? And have we won?

Of course not. Remember the coin toss? You flip as many times as necessary until it comes out, Heads, the developer wins.

This is a legal building site. Which means the owner has the right to build. If the DRB and the others turn him down, he's probably going to say, "I've got a legal building site. If you take away my right to build, pay me."

And the city will have to pay him. The architect/ owner paid $120,000 for the lot. He's spent a few thousand in engineer reports and the like. He'll want a little profit on his investment—time and labor, that sort of thing. And behind closed doors at City Hall, it will probably be negotiated. That's life.

But that's not so important. What's important is your fighting to save this site. Your voice can do it, for you, for the neighbors, for the fox and the water and the greenery and the open space. And you will have kept off the site another unneeded house.

It's worth it.

May 9, 2003

Landslide!

The barking of dogs gave the first hint something was amiss. I ignored it, thinking, "There's a coyote out there," and fell back asleep. The time was around 5:30 on a May morning.

At that time, Adele Pitts stood in the kitchen of her Meadowlark home in Bluebird Knolls, preparing food for her dog. After she'd fed the dog she would dress and go off to work. But not this morning. She heard a rumbling sound and looked out her kitchen window.

The garage had disappeared.

She shook her head, knowing she could not have seen what she saw.

Then came a knocking on her door, and the loud voices of her neighbors.

"Mrs. Pitts! Mrs. Pitts! You have to come out!"

"Just as soon as I feed the dog," she said.

"You come out right now!"

She put down the dog's food, and wrapped in a bathrobe and wearing her slippers she left the house. She took ten or twelve steps when she heard a louder rumble. She turned.

This time her house disappeared.

Adele Pitts's house on Meadowlark was one of twenty-three houses that fell down that May dawn, twenty-five years ago. Another twenty-five were so crippled by the moving earth they had to be demolished. Forty-eight houses in all lay in groups of broken timber and shards of cement. When Bonnie and I visited the scene the next morning, the feeling was one of pity. How could a person's home be so reduced? Just a few broken boards, most in a single loose pile, others strewn about like an abandoned game of pick-up-sticks.

On that second morning, Charlie Boyd stood at a table, next to Salvation Army workers with their cups of coffee. Charlie was lining up volunteers to go down to an assigned address and try to gather whatever personal effects could be found. A letter, a wristwatch, a broken doll. Collect them, place them in a box with the address of the property. Not that property lines meant much. The earth had moved them. The hill was gone. Bluebird Knolls had been flattened.

Dale Ghere will tell us more about the landslide, how and why it happened, at the Historical Society meeting at City Hall in a few days. My own mind goes back to Adele Pitts, whom Bonnie and I knew. She had four children, grown and flown by the date of the disaster. Mrs. Pitts always asked about our son Steve and our daughter Laurel, were they studying, were they well? A lovely lady, Mrs. Pitts.

She was the only black living in Bluebird Knolls, with her dog (who turned up well 24 hours later). Mrs. Pitts, as we all called her, was a domestic worker. She cleaned houses. She lived in a house bought for her by her son John. Let me tell you about this family, one of the noble families of Laguna history, right up there with the Thurstons, the Ramseys, the Jahrauses.

She had four children, Esther, John, Elye, and little Adele. Esther was a slender, bright, beautiful woman. She helped start the Laguna Beach Interracial Citizens' Committee, of which I was the chair. She became the first president of the local chapter of the NAACP, interested in finding jobs for blacks in the community. Blacks then lived in two enclaves, one in the cottages on Ocean Avenue, from where Anastasia is now to where Café Zinc is now. The second enclave lived in rented houses in Laguna Canyon, along Woodland Drive and

Canyon Acres. Perhaps thirty families in all. Where have they gone? Driven out by high rents, no jobs, community indifference.

Mrs. Pitts stayed. Her son John stood 6-5 and weighed 210 pounds. He ran the 100 in ten seconds. He led the high school basketball team in scoring. But it was football where he truly starred. He played both ways, wide receiver on offense, linebacker on defense. After his graduation from college, the Buffalo Bills made him their first-round pick in the NFL draft. With the hefty signing bonus he bought a house for his mother. John spent ten years in the NFL. He became a banker in Scottsdale, Arizona. He has since retired. His brother, Elye, received his Ph.D. in International Relations from Stanford. Young Adele—I don't know. She ran track at Laguna High, went on to college. We've lost contact since.

Esther was the one we were closest to. Our son Steve was hopelessly in love with her. Who wasn't? Her real name was Queen Esther, and she looked it, regal and serene. I remember when Esther spoke to the Board of Realtors, trying to drum up jobs for blacks. After she finished, a realtor said to me, "I'd hire her in a minute," and I said, "Good. A typist? An agent?" "Oh, no," he said. "She can clean out my office after work every day." Today those thirty families of blacks are gone. In their place, if we think racially, are a few UCI profs and other professionals. The blue-collar blacks are gone.

Adele Pitts stayed. She had her house rebuilt on Meadowlark Lane. She didn't have to work, but she did. Finally she grew sick and died.

As the anniversary of the landslide approaches, I think of the tragedy, yes, but I think more of the other, societal tragedy. A community of blacks we could not absorb into the greater community of this town that prides itself on its diversity. I see Mrs. Pitts as she went off to work in the morning to clean yet another white family's house, a house unbroken by any landslide, undisturbed by any social trauma.

The dogs were right that morning. Something had been amiss.

June 20, 2003

Here's Your Hat…What's Your Hurry?

When I was a kid in the Bronx during the so-called Great Depression (I've always wondered what was so great about it) we would sometimes see people evicted from their living quarters. They'd huddle in pathetic clumps of humanity with their few sticks of furniture. They'd been evicted. They'd wait for Uncle Jake or Aunt Minnie to come along in the old jalopy to take the family in, two or three families living in one apartment, perhaps two bedrooms total. Sad stuff, no matter how you sliced it. No jobs. No food. No rent money. No *nada*. Take 'em away.

I have a soft spot for evictees. And I know how Uncle Jake or Aunt Minnie must have felt. We had a great-aunt Clara, a tiny lady in a black dress and one eye. She'd lost the other eye to cancer some years before. She hid the slitted eye socket, sewn shut, behind smoked glasses. She moved in with us when she could not live alone. While she lived with us, in a back room no bigger than a closet, she made patch quilts. My brother and I slept under her patch quilts for years and years. When I went into the Army a dozen or so years later, my quilt was packed away and somehow was lost. I still miss it. Aunt Clara lived with us for a year or so before moving on to another relative. She lived into her nineties. I'd read her the comics on Sundays. She was a great audience, laughing at the Katzenjammer Kids or what went on in Gasoline Alley. She'd laugh and wipe her weeping eye with a lace handkerchief, always so daintily, so lovely, so lovely.

So I'm a softy about people who suddenly are homeless. You know what? I can't work up a teary eye over the tarrying residents of El Morro Trailer Park.

Not a sob in my throat. Not even a long sigh. To me, an evictee has maybe three days to wait for Aunt Minnie to show up. The people of El Morro have had twenty years, plus five more, and now they want another thirty.

They've got a deal they want to ease past us. Let them stay those thirty years more and they'll turn over their units when they die to people who need affordable housing. Such a deal! It's not their units to turn over. It's ours. It's part of the park. The park owns the land. Which means the people own the land. Which means you and I own the land. I don't know about you, but I'm not giving up those units for housing.

Yes, we need more affordable housing units. But not in the park. If they can build housing units in the park at El Morro, why not a few such units on Main Beach Park? A whole cluster of them at the Montage? Hey, how about that? Build cheap units in the park at the Montage and invite in people from Santa Ana, to live cheek-by-jowl with the soon-to-be residents of those $4-million estate lots. That one I'll buy! For that I'd burn all my No on A & B placards!

You see how ludicrous this all is? A park is for people to come and park out.

A living unit is for people to come and live in. To each his own. That's why you can't turn your R-1 home into a bowling alley, open all night.

All right. We need housing units. The guy whose wacky brainchild this proposal is—to build housing units in the park—lives in The Club at Laguna, a modest-priced apartment complex off El Toro Road, in one of the three hundred units. Nice place. Well run. Clubhouse. Pool. Tennis court. Yes, it's out on El Toro Road but it's in the city of Laguna Beach. I know. Bonnie and I lived in The Club for five months while we renovated our house on Santa Cruz Street. It took me six minutes to drive from the apartment to City Hall. And you don't have to wait for someone to die to move in. There are always some units available at the Club. The rents aren't bad, for Laguna. Maybe $1150 for a small unit, up to $1650 for a good-sized one. You have some six, eight, ten firefighters or cops or schoolteachers or city employees who now live in Aliso Viejo but would rather live in Laguna Beach. The Club can put them up. No need to use up park land. If the city has to subsidize the rent a couple of hundred bucks for the really needy, let's do it.

And keep the park for the people. Evictees I weep over. The homeless we took in and learned to love and laugh with. I used to read the comics to my Aunt Clara and we'd laugh together. Nobody has to read the comics to the riders of the gravy train at El Morro Trailer Park. They've had twenty years past the eviction notice, plus five more. Now they want another thirty. They *are* the comics!

Time's up, guys. Here's your hat. There's the door. What's your hurry?

July 18, 2003

The World of Errata

While setting my column two weeks ago, the *Indy*'s computer crashed. I don't know what that means, but I assume all you techies do. If a computer crashes and nobody hears it, does that mean it didn't happen? It happened all right. So here is my [July 4] column with the truncated paragraph restored.

Losses come in all shapes. We've lost a piece of a hill in South Laguna. It will be replaced by a monster house. The City Council has denied an appeal by South Laguna neighbors. The house will measure 11,000-plus square feet, with a garage that can accommodate twenty-two cars. The hill will lose 9,000 cubic yards of earth, some say as much as 16,000 cubic yards.

We have an anti-mansionization ordinance. Now we will have a mansion. The council knows how to keep things in balance, right?

There. Now for correcting the rest of the world.

Computers crash and gremlins take over. In last week's *Indy* on the history pages, the paper published a piece about somebody named Don Williams. Ain't no such person. The gremlins removed the last two letters. It's Don Williamson, architect, former executive producer of the Pageant, outspoken member of the Festival of Arts Foundation, and nearly ninety, an active owner of a business that makes games for theme parks.

Don is one of Laguna's true Renaissance figures. He lives atop Bluebird Canyon in a house he designed and built after the fire had taken his and Jo's house in Temple Hills.

Don lives alone, goes to work every day, fights all the good fights to keep Laguna modest and beautiful. He fought to keep the Festival and Pageant here in

Laguna. His days with the Pageant were its glory days and years; each tableau so meticulously crafted, lit, and produced as to raise performance art to new levels.

Laguna Beach Festival of the Arts

Don has fought off adversity as well. Wife Jo, one of the great beauties of Laguna, suffered a series of strokes. When their house burned down, a photographer captured a shot of Don and Jo, amid the ashes, looking at each other, their faces a mix of tragic loss and fugitive hope. Jo has since died. Don's son and partner at work, Doug, died of a hideous flesh-eating virus that took him away in less than 24 hours, leaving his heartbroken wife, Kathi. Don's daughter Jenny, a Sawdust artist for years, suffered a crippling stroke; she still fills her booth with astonishing art. Jenny's husband, Geoff Riker, lost an eye to an exploding champagne bottle; later he would die of a painful liver failure.

Don carries on. Survivor.

Last week Francie Holder, on the history pages, asked a question in print—is it true that Harrison Ford actually appeared on the Laguna stage where Hollywood biggies discovered him? Francie asks: Is it true or is it urban legend?

It's true, Francie. A local play reviewer singled out the young man making his debut in *John Brown's Body*, the Civil War poetic drama by Stephen Vincent Benet, and praised his acting. An agent came to see and a career was launched. I know. I wrote the play review.

I love Francie's column and its title, given her by brother Rich Holder, "Little Known Facts of Even Less Value." Here's another fact. Cleo Street is misspelled. It should be Clio, one of the Muses. After all, we have Thalia and Calliope, two Muses. It has to be Clio, Muse of History. Perhaps the Arts Commission could foster a campaign to place classic statues of the Muses at the entrance to each of our Muse streets.

We need to honor our history. We have once again a Festival of Arts board that would wipe it out for a few bucks. It wants to permit other communities to copycat our Pageant, pay us for the rights and stage their own living tableaus. Will it make us money? I'm not sure. People in those other communities who used to come down to Laguna for the day to buy art, eat out, go to the beach, and see the Pageant would be able to stay home and attend the nearest copycat version.

And the signs at the entrances to our town will have to read:

Laguna Beach
Home of the Festival of Arts
Pageant of the Masters
and
Road Show Licensing Bureau

August 1, 2003

Aside from the rhetorical "Whoever told you you were a writer?" the one question I am most often asked is "What brought you to Laguna Beach?"

The short answer, "Blind luck," is also the truth.

When Bonnie and I piled into our new Ford sedan on July 1, 1955, together with our eighteen-month-old daughter, Laurel, and our six-month-old beagle pup, Cleo, and eight suitcases in the trunk, we had never heard of Laguna Beach.

Our adventure was simple: we were leaving New York for who knows where.

I had quit a job as editor of a line of paperback books a year earlier. I decided to freelance. During the past year I had sold a few short stories, a Western novel, and a book about a single ball game.

Our itinerary was directed in large part by the presence of our dog. At our side in the front seat of the Ford was a book, *Traveling with Bowser*, which listed all the motels along the way that would put up dogs. So our first night at Carlisle, Pennsylvania, was not to honor Jim Thorpe's college days, but because the town had a motel for Cleo.

So it went, with the child and the pup in the back seat, throwing up together or alternately, in one of those Port-A-Cribs that people used for kids on long-distance trips, a kind of playpen that fitted the backseat (and served as a crib at night) where the two inhabitants played with each other for the next several thousand miles.

We made an unscheduled stop in Chicago. Laurel was a celiac baby—she could eat virtually no food with the exception of a few dabs of cottage cheese and a formula Bonnie prepared every night for the next day's intake. We were traveling in what turned out to be one of the hottest summers in America's history, in a car without air conditioning. (Few cars in 1955 had air conditioning.) Laurel started complaining one day, and when we touched her forehead, she singed our fingers. We found Chicago's Children's Hospital, where a doctor treated her and sent us on our way. Laurel was fine the next day. Kids do that, as you parents all know.

A trip to Bonnie's mom in Sioux City gave us a month to recoup. I spent some of the time in the town's barbershop because it was air-conditioned. The outside temps were often over 100. At the old house where Mama lived I found an empty attic with room for a chair and my portable typewriter. Sitting in my under-drawers, I wrote a Western. While in Sioux City we received a telegram from a friend in New York that my book, *A Day in the Bleachers,* had been well received by the *New York Times* and the *Herald Tribune* (the *Trib* had given it a full-page rave). So I knew I had made the right career change. (The book sold six hundred copies.)

We went on. In North Platte, Nebraska, I took Cleo out for her last nighttime wee-wee, and she encountered the prey of all hunting dogs, a jackrabbit. Except this jackrabbit stood six feet tall, a stalwart in the moon-lit night, eyeing this pathetic pup the way King Kong eyed Fay Wray. With the good sense of a New York-born and -bred beagle, Cleo pretended she didn't know the rabbit was there and was thoroughly delighted when I arrived back at the motel room, where she promptly peed on the motel rug. We left very early the next morning.

Outside of Santa Fe, on Route 66, the car suddenly blew its right front tire and buried its nose in a shale hill. A friendly car stopped and helped change the tire and we were off again, battered but unbowed. Laurel and Cleo slept through the blowout and tire change.

In California we stopped for a week with Bonnie's sister Lil and brother-in-law Harry in Pacoima, in the Valley, and then we went on, still not knowing where we'd finally pull up and say, "Ah!" On our way down the coast toward San Diego, where we mooch with friends (we're big on mooching), we passed this small town that looked—well, it looked different from the other towns we had seen. Cute is the quick word, but it was and is more than cute. Fresh. Original. With a kind of look-at-me, ain't-I-the-cat's-meow air. In San Diego we asked our friends about this small town. "Oh, yes, Laguna Beach," they said. "A nice town."

"Is it expensive?" They paused. "No," one of them said. "Too many starving artists live there."

We drove back, stopped at the Chamber of Commerce, and asked for the name of a recommended realtor. "We're not allowed to recommend a realtor," we were told. So instead they handed us a list of three realtors. We went to the first, one Helen Bailey. Ms. Bailey, a handsome redhead of indeterminate age, took us to see a three-bedroom house for rent on Goff Street, and we moved in for $85 a month.

We've been here ever since. No, not on Goff Street. Two months later Helen Bailey came by with another rental, this time on the end of Jefferson Way in Bluebird Canyon. We were discovering not so much Laguna Beach but our own identities. I had been a New Yorker all my life, all the mean streets, all the noise and buzz and concrete canyons. Bonnie had been an Iowa girl who needed more sophisticated surroundings than afforded by Sioux City. Together we found a village. And discovered we were villagers.

Laguna had 6,000 people then. The population was three Republicans for one Democrat but we knew quality would prevail. We walked barefoot that first summer and fall. I swam every day in the Pacific, right through New Year's. I killed a rattlesnake on our kitchen deck on Jefferson Way, the snake pointed out to us by Cleo, our now intrepid hunter of small prey. With a hoe, I cut off the snake's head and mailed the rattles back to an editor friend in New York. Our nearest neighbor on Jefferson Way, Mary Zava, had a horse. Laurel would ride on Glissanda's bare back. We all picked mustard greens on a nearby hill; Bonnie boiled them for our vegetable.

An invisible weight on my back lifted. I was home.

Bonnie Hano shortly before the Hanos came to Laguna Beach

September 12, 2003

"Urbicide"

A few years after arriving in Laguna Beach, I decided the English language needed a new word. So I invented it.

Urbicide.

The murder of a city.

For some reason, none of the Webster boys or any other lexicographer picked up on it. Pity.

I liked the word then. I like it more today. Its homonym, herbicide, adds a pun-like quality to my word. Each sound-alike enumerates a killing. Urbicide—the murder of a city. Herbicide—the murder of plant life.

Back then, the reason for the word was an imminent threat posed by a freeway scheduled to run right down our Main Street, Coast Highway, which most villagers called The Boulevard.

The Boulevard would be lost, drowned beneath a swath of concrete poured over our major downtown artery. It was a threat not unlike the more recent one of a commercial airport at El Toro. In a sense, it was worse. This dagger struck right through Laguna. The city would be dead on the freeway's arrival. Urbicide.

So we fought for our life, and won, and the wannabe freeway died.

Today we find another case of urbicide in the making. This time it is the murder of South Laguna. Right off, I admit to a case of hyperbole. No, South Laguna would not be completely killed off. Just transmogrified into something very different, something very awful. In the foreseeable future it will be unrecognizable.

Right now South Laguna gives off the sense of small-town America at its finest. Tiny houses on narrow streets, private streets many of them, owned and maintained by the residents. The whole area issues an aura of gentleness, quaintness, smallness. Street signs are tacked to trees, if you can find them at all. It is yesterday, come alive.

Now much of South Laguna is a parking lot. What a cruel change! It is a swamp of vehicles owned by people associated with the monster resort across the highway. The present owners and managers of Montage must be held responsible for the concrete quagmire, if I may mix my analogies, and why not, it's my column.

But the city of Laguna Beach itself stands partly culpable. The city manager and others under his command joined with Treasure Island owners to low-ball the estimates on parking needs. Was this deliberate or just stupidity? Either way, culpability remains. A solution was apparent, way back then. Make the Treasure Island owners and operators keep to their written word of providing sufficient parking right on site. They failed to do so. The city refused to make them do so. Twin culpability. It became a question of demand and supply. Everybody concerned underestimated the demand for parking. The supply offered, on site, turns out to be totally insufficient. Yet there still remains a solution. When I wandered—that's me, just wandering—on a recent Sunday and saw all those empty estate lots, it appeared clear that parking could still be provided. There is the usual caveat. The owners of these estate lots must agree to give up a couple and convert them to an underground parking structure. Yes, the lots would otherwise sell for $4-million each—some say, $6-million—but that's just tough. The promise to provide sufficient parking on the premises remains in force, and it remains, right now, violated. Nor is the construction of my parking structure enough to solve South Laguna's problem. It helps, but more must be done.

Montage's employees must be persuaded to give up their cars to go to work. Or they can park their cars at ACT V and take shuttles to work. Carpooling must be encouraged—and if employees refuse to take advantage of such an arrangement, carpooling should cease to be an option and instead become a mandate.

Even these steps will not totally clear the streets. But they will help. South Laguna must be saved. It is the last place on earth one would turn into a parking lot. The City Council must be made to understand this. We who would save the village must come out and say so, again and again. We have been ignored. The parking lords still dominate the town. But that can be changed if people begin to demand the change. The owners of Montage keep telling us how well they are doing, how terrific is the occupancy rate, and therefore how great will be our take from bed taxes. Yes, in three or four years, we'll have the money, they tell us. Well, three or four years are more than enough to kill a hunk of South Laguna.

The Montage owners insist they have a solution. They'll buy the property across the street, next to Ruby's, and turn it into a parking structure. Never mind that the strip of land is too small for an adequate structure. Never mind that the strip of land is zoned "recreational." Zones can be changed, they know. They know how easily such a change can be achieved, with the present city government. And we'll have a new form of recreation. Call it Bumper Cars. Perhaps Disney can be persuaded to build and operate it.

Until any of this can occur, Montage employees keep racing across the highway, to work or to their cars. That too is a recreation. Run for Your Lives.

Meanwhile, South Laguna is dying.

December 24, 2003

Peace

In the midst of recall infighting and rancorous debate, amid the hurly burly of local melees from Driftwood to the Festival of Arts, in the arena of fights over views, hedge heights, and dog feces on the beach, we sometimes lose sight of the greater world around us, where the real wars are going on. It is surprisingly easy to lose sight. There are days, for instance, when I cannot find a word about Israel and the Palestinians on the first pages of the *Los Angeles Times*; heck, it has been weeks, if not months, since I've read a word about Ireland and its "troubles."

Yet war continues.

American boys die nearly every day in Iraq. Fighting goes on in Indonesia and the Philippines; it threatens to break out anew in India and Pakistan. Iran is or is not building a nuclear bomb. North Korea is, period. And where there is a story about Israel, it usually reads: "Road map to peace is derailed."

Yet one fact may be discerned in all this blood-shedding and clash of swords. Of the near-seven billion people alive on the planet today, only the smallest fraction of that number is engaged in killing its neighbors. War remains an aberration. Once I fought in a war. I did so willingly. Today I am a peacenik. I am so willingly. Peace is my flag, my banner. Shalom!

When friends argue with me about my optimism over peace, I must recite one other fact: Not counting the wars that go on today, every war that has ever been fought has come to a peaceful end. Look at who are some of our allies today: Japan, Germany, and Italy. Our cold-war combatant, Russia, is now an ally, if not a friend. Peace takes over. Not always a lasting or well-received peace. Nearly always an uneasy peace. But every war, sometime, somehow, ends. Every one.

You remember the Mau Mau uprising in Kenya some decades ago? Violent bloodthirsty Kenyan natives murdered white English settlers—Kenya was a British colony, then—and for four years the killing and rape and pillage raged. It appeared nothing would stop the blood-letting. Then the British, tired, bloodied, discouraged (you may fill in the blank), decided enough was enough. They withdrew from Kenya.

The war ended. Like that.

I believe, for instance, if Israel removes its settlements and agrees to a specific date to permit and approve of a Palestinian state, that war will sputter out and die.

Remember the mantra: All wars end.

It is not that war is inevitable. It is peace that is inevitable.

No, I do not expect to see an all-inclusive peace in my lifetime. Perhaps not in my son's lifetime—he is after all, 59 years old. But in his daughter's lifetime, my granddaughter's lifetime? Yes, I believe so. It will come.

It may not be by legislative fiat, national or international. It may only be a sense of—enough is enough. We are blood-dry. We are sick of killing each other. People may decide this matter. And leaders will follow. If they do not, well, we'll just recall them. Or not elect them. Or not reelect them.

Peace will become the major issue in election times, here and elsewhere. Not on television, perhaps. But in home and hut. We must lay aside guns, bombs, poison gases. We must stop killing each other. If for no other reason than it seldom works. Killing begets killing. And we must stop it. War is an aberration. It is sickness.

Most of the near-seven billion people on this planet are healthy and well, or at least not afflicted with war-sickness. And those near-seven billion people will prevail.

No, we won't love each other. We don't love each other today. Democrats don't love Republicans. Whites don't love blacks. Nobody loves Barry Bonds. Love is not on the table here. It is hate and killing and war. I don't know what causes war. Surely it is not the simplistic cause people so easily give: hunger, poverty, and disease. Sometimes yes, other times no. Benjamin Franklin, George Washington, and Sam Adams were neither hungry, poor, nor sickly. Yet they started a war against the British. Wars have different causes, and to study them, which we must do despite the hymn "We ain't gonna study war no more," will take time and money and fine minds. But we have history to draw from.

Every war ends. Why does it end? How does it end? Study and learn how peace evolved. Or don't study it, and it will evolve anyway. No, it won't likely evolve from wars or terrorism or from wars of any sort. Wars beget wars. Violence begets violence. People do not like killing each other. Put it another way: war is always a mistake. Someplace along the road to peace, a mistake was made by one side or the other or by both.

When we read in the paper that Bush's road map to peace is a failure or has been derailed, don't believe it. The press must sell newspapers. War sells. Peace, alas, doesn't. But all road maps to peace are worth pursuing. The map will hit cold trails. It will have to be redrawn. It probably won't be Bush's map that gets us there but somebody else's. It will happen.

Peace? Smell the wind. It's coming.

January 16, 2004

Liberal

We are entering the political campaigns here in Laguna and throughout the nation. Men and women will come forward to ask for your vote. They will try to define themselves. Sometimes they are not fast enough; others barge in and define candidates for you. And one word will be heard and bandied about, treated as a dirty word, something to be ashamed of, something to be held in contempt.

Liberal.

Although I admire the art of Michael Ramirez, cartoonist for the *Los Angeles Times*, I abhor his politics. Take a recent Ramirez cartoon as an example. We see John Kerry at the Democratic convention, at the lectern, trying to define himself. And as he utters his words of definition—veteran, prosecutor, senator, whatever—Ramirez has decided to define him his way. Behind Kerry on the huge television screen, the word *Liberal* screams out at the audience. There. Take that, John Kerry. No matter what you say, Michael Ramirez knows better. You...are...a...LIBERAL.

If I were John Kerry, I would 'fess up. You bet I'm a liberal. And, if I were Kerry, I'd say, "I have two words for those who don't like it."

Abraham Lincoln.

Lincoln was a liberal. A uniter. A man who favored labor over capital. A man who freed the slaves. A liberal.

If he needed more, I'd offer Kerry two more words.

Teddy Roosevelt.

He fought the big bosses. He was the first president to tax corporate finances. He fought the mining industry when it wanted to dig up the Grand Canyon. A trust-buster. A liberal.

133

It may seem odd, but they were both Republicans.

Liberals can be of any political shade if they also believe in advancing the right of the little guy, of the disadvantaged, the underrepresented. Once blacks were measured in the Constitution as worth three-fifths of whites, for the purpose of counting Americans. Once women couldn't vote. Liberals changed that. Once we had no social security, no Medicare. Liberals changed that. Would you roll back minimum-wage laws? Factory safety regulations? Clean air and clean water laws? Would you get rid of them? They were written by liberals.

Liberals kept hydroelectric dams out of the Grand Canyon. Liberals kept Disney from turning Mineral King into yet another Disney resort. Fair housing laws. Fair employment laws. Fair political practices. Liberals gave us all those.

Once factories employed children ten, twelve, fourteen years of age to work ten, twelve, fourteen hours a day. Liberals changed that.

In case you didn't know, I'm a liberal. Long before the Civil Rights Amendment of the 1960s, back in 1948, Bonnie and I went door to door in Harlem, registering blacks. When we came to Laguna in 1955, we discovered that black residents could not have their hair cut in Laguna barbershops. Bonnie and I and a handful of Lagunans, black and white, changed that. Liberals, all.

So let me define myself. I am a liberal, yes, but I am also a Democrat, a Jew, a combat veteran of World War II, an American. I put those terms in no particular order. I am other things as well: a writer who has been published in every decade since the 1930s, a former teacher, a former editor. I am a father and a grandfather. I am a husband.

None of these words can be used against me, except one. Liberal. I am a liberal. To those closed-minded people, the case is closed.

Well, I am opening the case. I refuse to permit you to define me in your terms. I refuse to permit you to use "liberal" as a pejorative. I insist you accept me, liberal voice and all. Would you brush aside that I have given 60 pints of blood to strangers, and will give more? Will you ignore that I coached Little League kids my first summer in Laguna? I still hold doors for little old ladies who probably are younger than I.

So look at your candidates. Listen to them when they define themselves. And know that they are more, far more, than a thoughtless prejudice would have you think. And if any of them is a liberal, by his or her definition, remember Abraham Lincoln and Teddy Roosevelt. If you insist on calling a candidate a liberal, that candidate should thank you. You have linked that candidate with Lincoln and Teddy Roosevelt and others who have made America what it is today.

Who needs greater glory?

February 6, 2004

Give Me Your Streets

Eric Jessen's erudite letter concerning the pronunciation and definition of Glenneyre (pronounced "Glen-air" and meaning "a field of daffodils without cows") may read like the last word, but another precinct has already checked in.

When Mike Phillips worked for a newspaper in this county some fifteen or so years ago, he decided to write a feature on Laguna's street names. With the help of Tallie Parrish, then of the Planning Department, he located a map, pre-1920, which showed him Glenneyre Street. Except this map spelled it "Glennery," the phonetic spelling, apparently, of a not terribly literate cartographer.

Glennery, as in airy; not Glenneyre, as in air.

No, I don't think this will be the last, last word, either. These matters take on a life of their own. Perhaps Francie Holder can sic her researchers onto the hunt.

Speaking of street names, what is your favorite street here in Laguna? And why? I have two favorites, one for the way it sounds, and the other for the way it is hidden and suddenly comes up on you. Or me.

Just to say it, I love Glomstad Lane. What a name! No frills attached. No phony euphemism to make it what it isn't. Glomstad is an unexpected driveway off Wendt Terrace (another great name) leading to a collection of hidden houses. But who was Glomstad?

My other favorite street, regardless of name, is Palmer Place. You probably don't know Palmer Place; most people living within blocks of it have never heard of it. Drive up Bluebird Canyon from the Coast, and at Catalina you'll see a sign that reads: "No through street." Ignore it. Turn left and drive to the end, and turn right and you'll be on Palmer Place, on the very lip of Bluebird Canyon with a clutch of tiny houses, all jewels; one is aptly called Anne Hathaway Cottage, named after the equally hidden wife of Shakespeare.

I found Palmer Place when I was collecting money on Dollars for Democrats Day, an annual event long abandoned because it took too much time and brought in too little money. Now you just phone your favorite lobbyist and rake in the hundreds of thousands. I dug up my Democrats from a precinct list and found a woman living on Palmer Place. I stumbled upon the street, knocked on the door, and met this tiny old woman—in her late eighties—who invited me in, offered me a cup of tea (I hate tea, but I accepted it), and we chatted for a half hour or so. No wonder they say talk is cheap. She gave me a crumpled dollar, and every year for several years I returned for my dollar, my tea, and my tête-à-tête.

Glomstad Lane. "What a name! No frills attached."

My donor lived on Palmer Place into her nineties, then went into a retirement home and died at about a hundred. A lovely lady. I remember Palmer Place dearly. Village Laguna's Charm House Tour need not search all over town for houses; Palmer Place defines charm.

Some streets lose their names. What has happened to Whipple Way? It's been changed to something indistinguishable. Yet it was named after a local named Whipple, who in turn descended from a Whipple who signed the Declaration of Independence. We must not keep snipping ourselves free of history. Bring back Whipple Way!

And Johnson Street. Plain vanilla. Nothing fancy. Today it is Shadow Lane. Shadow Lane ought to be in Fountain Valley, where there is no fountain, and it sits in no valley, and used to be called Cow Town or something equally vivid. Then the cows left and the town needed a new name. Well, so does Shadow Lane need a new name. How about Johnson Street?

Streets. What are your favorite streets, and why? Let me know. I'm in the phone book, if you're a Luddite, like me. The streets of Laguna—Wildwood, Calliope, Fairywood Lane. Yours?

February 20, 2004

Favorite Streets: Final Episode

When I last wrote of my favorite streets in Laguna—
Glomstad Lane and Palmer Place—I had no idea who
Glomstad was and I still don't know who Palmer was or
is.

Now we all know Leif Glomstad (see his photo in
"The Laguna Home Companion" supplied by Dick and
Ann Frank). The photo stunned me. Once I learned
he'd come from Norway, I had pictured Glomstad as an
old man with a white billowy beard and a dour expression carved on his face from all those Norse winters.

Instead, think young Gary Cooper, Randolph Scott,
the rakish Jimmy Stewart before he learned to drawl.
Glomstad could have gone straight to Hollywood with
no fear that his Norwegian accent would impede his
path to stardom. The date of that photo is Christmas
1925, the time of the silent films.

Perhaps the smile comes from knowing about Laguna real estate values, even back then. Soon he would
build all the houses that filled Glomstad Lane—a tri-
plex, a duplex, and a couple of single-unit residences.
He built them all by hand, and his wife built all the
furniture. They lived at 625 Glomstad Lane until 1967,
when they sold the house to the Franks and moved into
Leisure World. The house is nearly eighty years old and
has had just two owners, the original builders and the
Franks. Love that sense of history.

And Palmer Place, at the edge of Bluebird Canyon.
I remember the old lady who used to serve me tea and
chit-chat and gave me dollars for Democrats—her last
name was Herron. No, I don't remember her first name.
I called her Mrs. Herron. Later there would be a Mark
Herron, appearing on the Laguna Playhouse stage do-

ing summer stock. A good actor, in the Montgomery Clift mode, but just a shade less effective. He became the fifth husband of Judy Garland. Was he related to Mrs. Herron? I wonder.

You voted for your favorite streets. Tim, up on Bluebird Knolls, likes the street he lives on. He likes its sound. "Flamingo," he says slowly, treasuring the syllables. "It rolls off the tongue." It is a cul-de-sac street, he reminds me, "with mind-boggling views." So score one for Flamingo, one of the birds-of-a-feather streets up on the Knolls, joining Meadowlark and Oriole in birdsong. (Do flamingos sing?)

Michael Hoag in a letter to the *Indy* favors "PCH and Broadway–Laguna Canyon Road." They lead cars out of town. Michael is our latter-day Jim Dilley in his dislike of the "infernal" combustion machine. He likes streets where people walk but cars can't run. Roosevelt Lane in the Canyon, six feet wide, is one of his favorites.

But I don't think there really is a street named PCH or even by its full name, Pacific Coast Highway. In Laguna, it's South Coast Highway, North Coast Highway, divided by Broadway. Actually it once was Boulevard, not Highway at all, so much the better name for the road we like to call Laguna's Main Street.

Let's crusade for a name change back to Boulevard. You can stroll on a boulevard; you can't stroll on a highway. They even write songs about boulevards—remember "The Boulevard of Broken Dreams"? Can you imagine a highway of broken dreams? Nah. Just broken axles.

Debbie Hertz casts a vote for a street I never heard of: Hedge Lane. About 500 feet long, she says, "a defiant little street that feels no need to comply with the city ordinances and is forthright about it. The sign for the turnoff has been hand painted on a piece of wood which sits in the brush at the turn. No fancy poles. Just the sign."

Debbie once lived on the corner of Wave and Cliff and liked the street. Today she's not so sure. "The mortality rate sounds a bit too high." The address? 911 Cliff.

I'd like to honor some of these streets. If there is a history to the street—like Glomstad Lane—put a plaque, with the story. The houses of Olympic Village, named after the 1932 Olympic Games heroes—Frank Wykoff, the Compton Comet, who was the first man, I believe, to run the 100 meters in 9.4 seconds; Blazing Ben Eastman; Babe Didrikson. Or those streets named after the Muses, Calliope, Thalia, the misspelled Cleo, how about a small statue done in classical style at the foot of each street?

Which leaves Montage Resort Drive. How shall we honor it? How about a No Parking Sign?

Christ Killer

During my growing-up days, we lived most of the
time in a first-floor apartment of a six-story building
on Montgomery Avenue in the Jewish neighborhood
of the Bronx. My brother and I shared a bedroom; my
folks had the other bedroom. Both bedrooms looked out
on the street. Because of an old family habit, we always
slept with the bedroom windows open. Winter, summer,
rain, snow, heat. Windows open.

It must have tempted the three kids who came
along one dawn. They saw the open window to my
folks' bedroom and, while two boys played lookout, the
third boy hoisted himself to the windowsill and grabbed
my mother's wristwatch. Had he reached 6 or 8 inches
farther he would have had my mother's diamond ring.
Today, instead, Bonnie wears it.

The three kids ran. The milkman saw them and
gave chase. He collared one of the boys. The other two
escaped, one of them with the watch.

The boy was taken into custody. He was twelve
years old, an Irish kid from below the cliffs on the west
side of the Bronx. My grandfather Ike was a cop. My
father had been a lawyer before his practice dried up
in the Depression. The two of them put pressure on
my mother to bring charges against the boy. The police
needed somebody to sign the arrest warrant. My mother was it. She didn't want to, but the conversation wore
her down. "He's a thief," my father said. "But he's just
a little boy," my mother protested. My grandfather was
a lieutenant in the police force in charge of a precinct
house in Brooklyn. He was, I believe, the highest-rank-
ing Jew in the New York Police Department. He was

my mother's father. When he was five years old, he had seen Lincoln in a parade. He had a Prussian's sense of black and white, with no grays between. "He committed a crime. He has to pay," he said. "What will happen to him?" my mother wanted to know. "He'll go to reform school."

And so, with reluctance, my mother agreed.

On Saturday morning, the apartment doorbell rang. It was the mother of the boy, crying. I was at home with my mother. My brother, Alfie, must have been playing with his friends. My father was out somewhere.

The woman pleaded her case. "He is just a little boy," she cried. "Like your boy there," pointing at me. I stood across the room. The woman—a little overweight wearing a flowery dress—sat in a chair across from my mother. The two women stared at each other, ten, twelve feet apart. "He's sorry. He won't do it again. We walloped him good. He's a good boy. He didn't mean it. It was the other two."

My mother said, "Why won't he tell us their names?"

The mother's lips came together, in a tight line. "I don't know their names." It was the code of the street. You didn't rat on your friends.

My mother refused to yield. No. She couldn't stop the charge.

And the horror began. The woman got down from her chair and fell to her knees. She began to creep forward on her knees, toward my mother. "Please," she kept saying as she crept closer. Finally she reached my mother's chair. "Please." She reached forward for the hem of my mother's skirt. "Please!" she said again. "Please!"

My mother pulled away quickly, and the woman slipped, falling face forward. From the floor, her head twisted up to my mother, she said "Jew bitch! Christ killer!"

She got up and brushed off her dress and walked to the door. She turned and said again, "Christ killer!" She left.

That night at the supper table my mother recounted the incident. My father listened quietly. My mother said, "I'm not going to bring charges against that boy." My father started to retort, but something in my mother's face told him it was no use. This was the final word. My mother would not file charges. The boy would go free.

Is there a lesson here? Had my mother just succumbed to blackmail? I like to think not. She was too tough for that. My mother was a tough cookie. She was the first of the bra burners. She'd remove her bra every spring and not put on a bra until fall. Somebody once asked her why. "Because I like the freedom," she said. No, she wouldn't let herself be blackmailed.

One Irish Catholic family believed the old rot of a blood curse on an entire people. My mother proved it wrong, cast it aside. She broke the chain of tit-for-tat. She cut herself—and the rest of us—loose from that filthy epithet, "Christ killer." She threw Jesus's words back at them: "Forgive them for they know not what they do." She forgave the boy. She forgave the mother. Were she alive, she'd probably forgive Mel Gibson.

Our windows remained open. Nobody ever reached in again and stole from us.

April 30, 2004

Peace Academy

What this country needs more than a good 5-cent cigar or the end to the designated hitter rule is a peace academy. A place where young people learn to wage peace.

We have war academies in abundance. Each year we send young men and women to each of the three major academies: West Point, Annapolis, and Colorado Springs. Total enrollment at each academy, as I write, is about 4,000 students. Those students at each academy undergo a rigorous curriculum, ending with BS degrees, military commissions, and obligations to give back five years of service to the Army or Navy or six years to the Air Force. They end up superb killing machines. Human beings, but ready to kill. I do not know what the washout rate is; I assume it is very high. This is a tough life. Perhaps each academy graduates 500 or 600 youngsters each year.

We have no peace academy. Nobody enters. Nobody graduates. There is a pale substitute for such an academy in Washington, D.C., called the Peace Institute. It has little relevance to the academy of peace that I envision.

Today we wage peace by the seat of our pants. It is a "by guess, by gosh" method. Today we call our occupation forces in Iraq or wherever "peacekeepers." They keep peace at the point of a bayonet.

We need something different. We need people trained in the methodology of peace to step in once the military phase is finished. Or before it has begun.

So I picture a peace academy with its 4,000 young men and women entering its doors to learn two things: what are the causes of war, and how does peace eventually come about. To boil it down to four words: why war, how peace.

One quick caveat. This is not a touchy-feely academy I am talking about. I do not see classrooms of young people sitting down and holding hands while they chant "Om."

What do I see? Students with computers studying wars. How they came about. A war was waged 12,000 years ago, the first recorded war. What was it? Who fought whom? And why? And how did it end? I see my academics studying all the wars of history—the Peloponnesian Wars, five centuries before Christ. Why did Sparta attack Athens, or was it the other way around? How did it end? Why war, how peace? We are told by pundits that wars are caused by hunger, disease, and poverty. Some surely are. Others aren't. How otherwise explain the American Revolution, with healthy, wealthy, and well-fed Benjamin Franklin, George Washington, and Thomas Jefferson, among others, leading the colonies into war against Mother England? The American Civil War. World Wars I and II. Vietnam. Rwanda. Sudan. The Wars of the Roses. The Hundred Years' War. Why? What caused those wars? What ended them?

When they have studied all this, my young men and women—peaceniks, people will call them; I prefer ambassadors of peace—will be sent off on their obligatory service period. I see them in our embassies and consulates around the world, particularly in the hot spots. What they will have learned may—fingers crossed—cool down a hot spot, abort a war before it begins. Or help bring peace once a war has started. Is there a better goal for any of us?

Or send them to our delegation to the United Nations. Or to Congressional staffs, adding a new expertise to the know-how arsenal of those legislators. Send them into professorships at colleges and universities to teach undergraduates all about peace. And perhaps in the process end a war not yet fought and perhaps never to be fought. Because of these peace ambassadors.

So that is my idea of the week.

Does it stand a chance? Does it sound too simple? Do we have the courage to suggest that peace no longer be trusted to war makers but rather to those who have studied war and why it comes about and how it sometimes ends?

What do you think? If you like the idea, how do we sell it? Or am I just, as usual, blundering?

May 14, 2004

Courting a Human Disaster

Remember when would-be workers raced across Coast Highway in front of four lanes of traffic? Remember when would-be workers waiting hours for a job offer had to relieve themselves, and hunkered over somebody's bushes to urinate? Remember when you drove up to the job center and the next thing you knew, you had a dozen people clawing at your car window, begging for work?

Compare all that to what exists today. Workers line up neatly. Employers don't have to peel past a dozen men who will take any job, just to make a buck.

Workers who are hired pay a dollar back to the Day Workers' Center; employers pay $5 for every job they hire. A chemical toilet is at the Center.

The Day Workers' Center in the Canyon is a hiring hall, and it works with the efficiency of a good watch. Look at it quickly, because its time may be up.

At the City Council meeting of May 4, the council majority voted down a request from the Cross Cultural Council, parent organization of the Day Workers' Center, for a measly $8,000 in order to keep going.

In order to give the group the $8,000, it would have been necessary to dip into the city's disaster reserve fund. How much money is in that fund? A mere $3.5 million.

Said the mayor: "I can't go into that fund. Suppose we have a disaster. That's what the money is for."

The mayor defines "disaster" in the narrowest terms. She thinks fire, flood, earthquake, landslide. We face a human disaster if the Day Workers' Center closes its doors and we are back to people risking their lives crossing streets; we are back to men urinating in the

148

bushes. We're back to those hordes of humans shouting to be hired. We're back to chaos.

Eight thousand bucks. The irony of it all is that it will cost thousands. City Councilmembers Toni Iseman and Steve Dicterow say it will cost thousands. The headline in last week's *Indy* said it would cost thousands. (And if you can't believe Stu Saffer, who can you believe?)

We spent fifteen times $8,000 to rebuild the rocket ship. We gave 120 times as much to Treasure Island when we waived the usual construction fees. We're great for padding the pockets of developers; we're even better at picking the pockets of the poor. To say nothing of the $8-million—not $8,000—overrun for the city park at Montage. Eight thousand dollars. Seven times as much was spent to get the mayor elected. Who's counting?

Nobody's counting. Except when it comes to saving money and closing down a hiring hall for people who have no political clout.

During the budget discussions just past, the Cross Cultural Council had asked for $34,000. The City Council agreed to $24,000 but also said, "Come back later, and we'll see what we can do about making up the difference." So the Cross Cultural Council came back, and the City Council gave it what for. A finger in the eye.

We're lacking $8,000 to keep the Day Workers' Center going. Sally Rapuano and David Peck, who have worked to exhaustion to keep the Center alive, throw up their hands. "We may have to close it down," they said the other day. Well, maybe they won't have to. Village Laguna has kicked in $1,200 to help cut the shortfall. It's a start. Can the city come up with a few bucks more?

What is the cost of averting a disaster? Or is urinating in the bushes the preferred alternative?

May 28, 2004

Memorial Day

I remember the day my brother's body arrived at a dock
on the Hudson River in Manhattan. My father and I had
gone down to the solemn ceremony that would follow;
we sat in a hastily put-together room outside the landing deck in company with some three hundred others,
all of whom had come to claim the bodies of their loved
ones, killed in World War II.

A day to remember. I think of it on Memorial Day
each year.

I remember how that ceremony went. An officer
stood and read off the names of each of the dead men—
all men, no women, a different time, a different war—as
we sat on folding chairs, waiting until he had finished
his sorrowful litany. All the names, in alphabetical order.
Then he finished and after a pause he looked out at the
room and said, "Now will the loved ones please rise."

The whole room rose, all of us, fathers, mothers,
brothers, sisters, wives, sweethearts, friends, all who
had been afflicted by a young man's death. And when
we all stood, my father and I looked at each other, and I
put my left arm around his shoulder, as he wept silently.
Alfie had been his first-born, and his namesake.

Perhaps the single worst moment in life is the death
of a child. Children ought not die before their parents.
Nature's scheme is uprooted, disrupted, even corrupted
by that death. It ought to be parents first, then children.

War destroys that order. War is the destroyer of
nature. Children die, and hundreds of other people, like
those in the room at the dock on the Hudson, are uprooted by those deaths and weep helplessly. Parents are
especially gutted. How could it not be?

I remember how protective Alfie and I had been of our parents when we were overseas in World War II. In the last letter I would receive from my brother, he wrote from his base in England after his thirteenth mission with the 8th Air Force as a bombardier in a B-17, "It's becoming very rough here, but for cripes' sake, don't tell the folks."

Of course I would not tell the folks. That was the unwritten rule. Oh, we would write to them about the rotten food in the mess halls, or drinking aged Scotch (sometimes even a month old!) on weekend passes, and all the hurry up and wait that marked our lives. And of course our parents knew war was no lark. Both of their sons had volunteered for service; neither of us had waited to be drafted. We went willingly, he to the skies over Europe, I to the islands in the Pacific.

Today I wonder with awe how they survived without shedding their sanity. Every day was like a new day of waiting, while we were in deadly skies or on the bloodstained sands. And every day they would wait for a letter, for word of death or injury. If no such word came, then they had their moment of relief. One more day had passed, and we were still alive.

On Memorial Days I do not think so much of the dead but rather of their parents, waiting, not knowing. Or finally knowing that their child had become a number.

Our parents partook of the war in their own ways. My father served on a draft board in Manhattan. My mother made bandages in the afternoons at the hospital in New York for the Red Cross and ultimately for some mother's son out there who may have been bleeding.

We speak of heroes of war. Yes, there are heroes. Men and women who serve honorably and with distinction. We seldom speak of those at home, the parents of members of the armed forces. Milton had it right: "They also serve who stand and wait."

Waiting at home in war is like a pause between breaths.

And so on this Memorial Day I set aside partisanship and plump for patriotism. Not just to honor those poor souls in Iraq, but for their parents at home, holding their breath. Perhaps one day we will put aside war—that destroyer of nature—and parents can breathe freely again.

That is my prayer, on this Day.

June 25, 2004

Whose Town Is It Anyway?

That was the headline of an ad that helped Carl Johnson win his Council seat some thirty years ago. The question still concerns me. Whose town is it, this village of ours?

If you travel south, you must find it hard to deny it is Montage's town. Montage owns Treasure Island, its hotel, its $3.5-million condos, its soon-to-be-built $8-million estates. But that is not enough to satisfy the hunger of huge developers. Montage also owns the old Ben Brown's. It owns Driftwood Estates. Rumor has it the Albertson's shopping lot is the next to go.

Look at the street sign over Coast Highway. Two signs, actually, one on each side of the highway. Each reads "Montage Resort Dr." I assume the "Dr." stands for Drive, not Doctor, but who knows?

The street signs disturb me. I could handle one sign, on the ocean side, directing motorists into the resort. But the sign on the other side directs motorists where? To Albertson's. To the Chabad. To SavOn. To the Reef Motel. Fantastic Sam's. Chinese Bistro. Z-Pizza. Animal Crackers. And the rest. None of which has any connection to Montage.

Or am I being naïve? It may indeed direct motorists who can't find parking at the resort and are beckoned to the shopping lot, which soon fills up daily with Montage's overflow vehicles. Perhaps you recall the City Council meeting of a few months ago, when councilmembers suddenly found steel in their spines and said to Montage, "You will park your vehicles on site. Not across the street. On site. We are not asking, we are demanding."

So for a day or two, the vehicles across the street seemed to thin out a speck. But just for a day or two. Now it is business as usual. "As usual" means streets awash with cars. Montage does what it wants. And City Hall genuflects.

That's South Laguna. Now look at downtown. Whose town is it? The sign on the wall at the post office suggests the answer is a Los Angeles real estate developer. Was I the only person in town who thought the parking lot at the post office was a city lot, for use by residents schlepping packages to be mailed? Turns out it wasn't a city lot at all. It belongs to an L.A. developer, who has redone the parking at the post office, so the schlep is sometimes quite a bit longer. That's not all. Now the developer has removed the newspaper racks at the post office. I am a newspaper headline looky-loo. I am a junkie, I need my fix of newspapers. I had a full cornucopia at the post office wall. The *L.A. Times*, the *Register*, the *Wall Street Journal*, *USA Today*. Even, at times, the *New York Times*. Plus all those freebies—this paper, the other so-called local papers. I could pick up my free copy of *OC Weekly* to continue my lusting over Commie Girl.

All gone. The developer shrugs off criticism of the move. It is his lot, he insists, and he is right. He says he doesn't have to keep the papers there. And he doesn't.

Talk about a good neighbor! And the same developer owns the Lumberyard, up to and including Cedar Creek Inn.

We are now talking a huge swath of downtown in one company's hands. That is how a town becomes a company town. It is here I take my stand. Laguna must not become a company town. We are not Irvine. I fear bigness of this sort, this village in one person's hand, in one corporation's boardroom, in one absentee landlord's profit-and-loss statement. I fear the loss of identity. Laguna's sense of self is linked with smallness. We rejoice in the Mom and Pop shops, in our low-rise profile. We don't want to lose that small-town flavor that makes Laguna Laguna. We call it the Pottery Shack. Not the Pottery Palace. If the pots are ever removed, will the site look like the old Shack? Or will it be just another shopping center? Will the site have its old identity? Or will it be Thoroughly Modern Mall-ie?

I don't know the answer to these questions. I am not against private ownership. I have thrived in a capitalistic society. I would not have it any other way. But I do know size counts. Bigger is not only not necessarily better; it may often be worse.

So I end where I began this essay: Whose town is this? Is it the residents' town, where we make the decisions? Or do we cede power to the already too powerful? If you agree that we must hang onto our town, be prepared to do so with tooth and claw. Or the town will disappear beneath the blade of a bulldozer and the heel of an out-of-town boot.

Such is the hunger of those who must have more.

October 1, 2004

The Thankless Job

People keep telling me that the most "thankless" job in Laguna Beach is serving on the Design Review Board.

I disagree. My tenure on the DRB back in 1972 and 1973 provided me with two years of grand fun, with a bit of payola thrown in. After we had granted Swensen's Ice Cream Parlor a variance for its building on Broadway—alas, long gone—Swensen's management promised us it would stay open until our meetings ended. The result was a twofold success. We conducted our business in two or two and a half hours, which included no time limit on public input—and we seated ourselves at Swensen's by nine o'clock or so, which did not put them out. And the chocolate sundaes were free. No wonder they went broke.

Let me tell you how I landed that "thankless" job. For one thing, I never applied for it. The Board of Adjustment used to hear all variances. Back in 1971, the council decided to replace the current board with three new members. The council met in closed session—nowadays it would have to be open to the public—and Mayor Richard Goldberg asked for three recommendations. Councilmember Pete Ostrander nominated fellow architect Chris Abel. Councilmember Ed Lorr nominated fellow arch-conservative, realtor Milt Hanson. And Roy Holm, in a moment of whimsy, nominated me. Mayor Goldberg said, "Fine. Three openings. Three names. Period."

The next morning Roy Holm phoned. "Congratulations," he said. "You've just been appointed to the Board of Adjustment."

"What's that?" I asked.

"You'll find out," Roy said airily. "You start next week."

Later I would characterize the board as one architect, one realtor, and one token human being. Chris Abel chaired the board. I was vice chair. Milt Hanson provided the comic relief when I wasn't holding a blueprint upside down, wondering why I couldn't find the front door. Milt had learned that Chris Abel's real name was—is—Ib Christian Abel. "What's with this 'Ib'?" Milt wanted to know. "First base?"

In 1972 the council decided to expand our jurisdiction to include design review. The ordinance, which I helped craft (Pete Ostrander wrote most of it), was scarcely dry when we began our reviewing. We added two new members, landscape architect Peter Weisbrod and long-time Festival of Arts exhibitor Lu Murphine (now Lu Campbell), whom I had recommended. Why not? She was bright, she knew and could apply the principles of design, and she was good-looking. (She still is.)

Once the City Council decided it wanted to meet with us in joint session. My mother had taught me early to stay out of joints like that, especially at night. We refused the invite. We had our mission, we had our work, we did it, and we didn't see the need to have the council looking over our shoulders.

Sometimes we made up law as we went along. I remember the problem Dave Monahan had. Dave owned a tiny piece of property at the corner of Cleo and Glenneyre on which he had built a tiny gem of a house people called Monahan's Castle. Maybe 850 square feet. Dave needed to add a small room, but to do so it appeared he would then need to provide a covered parking space. Which was impossible, if you followed the code. A garage or a carport would destroy that piece of land. We recalled that Dave had a couple of trees back there that bent together to form an arbor, a shelter of sorts. "Dave," we asked, "could you park your car under those trees?" "Sure," he said, and we had a solution. One of us said, "I don't know how the building code defines a 'covered' parking space, and I don't want anybody to tell me. As far as I'm concerned, Dave has a covered parking spot." And business went on.

Life on that first DRB was like that. We took chances. Laguna Federal Savings & Loan (where Wells Fargo now stands) needed more parking space. To get the space it needed, it would have to remove two buildings on the lot, the Barbara Weber Dance Studio and the Casa de Mandigo, two stories of apartments. Laguna Fed applied for and received a demolition permit.

We didn't like seeing those downtown buildings just disappear into a cloud of dust. There was no mechanism in Laguna to declare structures "historic" buildings. We decided our DRB was that mechanism. We passed a rush-through resolution declaring the buildings historic structures, and the Coastal Commission gave us a six-month reprieve to find new owners of the structures and to move them from the parking lot. Realtors Mark Gumbiner and Rick Balzer each took a building (for free). I thumbed through the Yellow Pages to help find a building mover. On two dawns, the buildings were relocated. Today the Barbara Weber Dance Studio is now the orthodontics office on Glenneyre, arguably the most handsome commercial building in town; the Casa de Mandigo is now the Royal Thai restaurant, with apartments above, on Coast Highway.

Just do it. That was our message. Nobody on the board worried whether we were loved or hated; nobody counted the number of people who thanked us or cursed us. I must say people still stop me in the street to remind me how I helped them with a design problem thirty-plus years ago. My mind being the sieve that it is, I have no recollection of that help. But I smile and say, "You're welcome."

So keep it up, DRB. You are doing a great job. The job today is much more difficult than it was back then. All those regulations. All those rules. And with the denial of a variance, there's a lawyer threatening to sue. Nobody is allowed to turn down a request to meet with the council. But otherwise, it's the same. Hear the applicant; hear the neighbors. Treat 'em all equally. And make your decisions. I know, I know. You have the mayor and the rest of the council majority fretting. You have an oversight committee studying you. Don't sweat it. You are the second-best DRB this town has ever seen. And I thank you.

4
It Takes a Villager
Laguna News-Post, 2005

August 4, 2005

Disaster tends to bring out the best in some people, the worst in others. There are those who dig in to help those in need. There are others who want to know how much it will cost and is it worth it.

Charlie Williams is the first type and one of the best of us all. He is the guy who went up the hill when the landslide struck and went to work, digging out people's possessions. One couple had lost their wedding rings. Charlie dove into the debris, some of which was half a house teetering over his head. He saw a glint. Found one ring. Figured the other had to be nearby. Had to crawl further under the teetering house. Found the second ring.

He doesn't talk about it. His wife does. She is proud. Why not? We are all proud of Charlie.

Then there are those who count the pennies first. The carpers and crybabies. We are hearing from them now. How expensive it is to live in Laguna Beach. What a time to bring that up! Of course it's expensive here. We spend money to support the arts, the community clinic, the library, our bus system. We buy open space. We guard our beaches and tidepools. We help provide a hiring hall out in the Canyon for the undocumented workers. We are a city that takes care of people.

I can't tell you how to find the money to solve the landslide problem. I don't know how. I just know it will come. I'm not against an increased sales tax. I'm not against a bond issue. We're good at working our way through disasters.

At the same time it's essential we look at how we construct the houses we live in. For years I've been a lone voice crying out for a new definition of "legal building site." Now Jane Egly has entered the arena. Many more will follow.

But mainly we'll keep our eye on the ball—the lives of those afflicted. We care for each other. Let the carpers and crybabies stay on the sidelines.

Back in the early 1960s, Bonnie and I built a house atop Bluebird Canyon, on a lot that was virtually vertical. A friend of ours, Fred Pratley, came by while the building had begun. He shook his head, said to us, "They're building on mud. You'll have to go deeper, find bedrock." He didn't say "mud," of course. He said a four-letter word, the color of mud.

So the builders went down, 10 feet, 15, 20, finally 26 feet. No bedrock. Fred Pratley, who was a geologist, said, "Build a steel and concrete foundation and tie the house to it." Which they did, and Fred—whom we paid nothing for his expertise, his advice—beamed. "Now you've got a bomb shelter," he said. "You're safe."

In 1968 we moved in. The rains came that next winter, into early 1969. Heavy rains. All around us, land moved and slid. Not ours. One night I heard a noise beneath the house, a kind of scraping sound. "An animal," I thought, "trying to stay dry." I fell back asleep.

Two days later I ran into Fred Pratley downtown. "Your house is holding up fine," he said.

"You!" I said. "That was you!" He'd heard the rain, got up at 2 a.m., drove to our house, and crawled down below to see how it was doing.

Today that house we no longer own still stands, through two landslides and more torrential rains. Fred Pratley is dead. He leaves a legacy in our hearts.

People like Charlie Williams and Fred Pratley make this town what it is. And it is the best town around. Of course we spend too much: because we want more.

It's not the only carping that goes on. The "illegal" aliens have become a favorite punching bag for people who like to hate. That's what I see when I read those letters and opinion pieces. The complaint has little to do with laws. It has much to do with prejudice.

My granddaughter, Chelsea Hano, who is 13, has written a poem about all this. She calls it "Prejudice Is…," and I run it below, with her permission:

> *Prejudice is just a thought in someone's head*
> *A thought that mixes with hate, anger, destruction and terror.*
> *Prejudice is a thought that causes violence and hurt.*
> *Tears and sorrow.*
> *Prejudice is an action against others' looks*
> *An action against those who differ.*
> *Actions bent on destruction and fear.*
> *Madness and pain.*
> *Prejudice is an emotion in someone's heart.*
> *A feel for destruction and a love for terror.*
> *Emotions that feed on death.*
> *Fear and rules.*
> *Prejudice is a word in someone's mouth*
> *A word that can start wars*
> *A word that is full of injustice*
> *Violence and horror.*
> *Prejudice is a lie in someone's soul.*
> *It eats you from the inside ridding you of love.*
> *A lie that all believe.*
> *No more lies!*

To those who would protect Laguna, expect to pay the price. The result, of course, is priceless.

Chelsea Hano, Arnold's granddaughter

September 1, 2005

On Sept. 1, 1955, Bonnie and I and our daughter, Laurel, and our beagle pup, Cleo, drove into Laguna Beach for the first time. We stopped at the Chamber of Commerce where we were handed a list of realtors. The first realtor on the list found us a house on Goff Street. We moved in that afternoon.

That was fifty years ago to this very day. I was thirty-three then; now I am eighty-three. Bonnie will be seventy-nine in a few days.

I had left a big city and its high density, its concrete walls, its thronged streets, its honking cabs, its nervous edge. If Chicago is the city of big shoulders, as Carl Sandburg says, then New York is the city of sharp elbows.

I had left a city and come to a village.

These days a subcommittee of the Planning Commission is busy rewriting parts of the Land Use Element. Across our computer has come a flutter of e-mails dealing with a controversy over the word "village." What does it really mean?

My advice to the subcommittee is: "Stop parsing."

Lift your eyes from your computer screens and look outside. That's village.

(All right, all right. That's smog, overcast, June gloom. Look outside on a nice day.) A city is big. A village is small.

A village is built to human scale.

A village has modest dimensions. It decries mansions.

A village has a leafy texture. A city feels of steel and stone.

This particular village smells of the sea and the earth. Manhattan smells of exhaust and soot.

The streets of a city are wide. Laguna's streets are narrow.

One day when returning from work in Manhattan, I saw a pack of rats crossing the street in front of me. One day in Laguna I saw a great blue heron crossing Glenneyre.

I remember when the city manager back in the 1950s came up Bluebird Canyon to elicit support for a ballot measure to include Bluebird Canyon in the city. Mary Zava, who lived with her husband, Bob, and her horse, Glissanda, on Jefferson Way, asked about street lights on her narrow gravel lane.

"Of course you'll get street lights," the city manager replied.

"We don't want them," Mary Zava said. So Jefferson Way had no street lights when it became part of the city.

Bonnie Hano riding Glissanda

Which doesn't make this village perfect. We march to our own cacophony. Where else would you find an Eiler Larsen standing at the corner of Forest and Coast Highway, saying hello to cars. One day I started across the street. Eiler boomed: "Hello, there. How are you-u-u?" "Fine, Eiler," I said, "and how are you?" "Don't argue with me!" he shouted back. Where else do you find a village this size, with three newspapers (but only half a bookstore)? Where else do you find a reverence of small cottages and Pyne Castle with its sixty-five rooms? Where else do you a find a dentist who used to live atop Bluebird Canyon and who skateboarded to work every morning? No, we are not perfect. We are villagers.

We have lost some of the village these past years. Once flocks of turkey buzzards filled our skies. The turkey buzzard is one of the ugliest creatures on earth, when it is on earth. In the sky, nothing is more majestic. One day a police officer had stopped her car near the top of Bluebird Canyon. She stood outside. I said to her, "What's going on?"

She pointed up.

Forty or so buzzards were wheeling through the air, their outstretched wings catching updrafts as they soared in unison.

"They do it once a month," she said. "They meet up there and spend an hour or so."

Together we watched the conclave in the sky. A few minutes after four they began to peel off.

"Home to nest," the police officer said.

The turkey buzzards are few these days, though the Laguna Canyon Conservancy folk tell me they are still here. Perhaps. But not in the numbers of yesteryear. I miss them.

I miss the foxes I used to see near the dip at Glenneyre. I miss the open hills now filled with houses. It's been at least thirty years since I've come across a king snake. And I miss the post–Labor Day Parade. We would go to the Sandpiper for a drink and then carry our glasses through the streets, stopping at every bar for a refill as we walked uptown, toasting the exodus of the summer tourists, a parade of Lagunans celebrating the return of Laguna to its villagers.

We would take our glasses home, to our nests.

Thanks for listening. Here's to the next fifty years. I'll drink to that.

5

Village Voices

Village Laguna Newsletter, 2005–2012

October 2005

Back in 1971, a geographer took a look at this community and wrote: "In many ways Laguna is an insult to technical progress and the twentieth century. The pace of life might find better accord in 1870 than in 1970. To some we are a roadblock to what is called progress. But in reality we are everyman's America. This village is different. To maintain our style of life we must maintain its difference." The geographer was and is Jon Brand, later the president of the Laguna Greenbelt and mayor of Laguna Beach. His words echo down the years. The twentieth century has given way to the twenty-first. We have entered a new millennium. And Brand's words ring true. We are everyman's America. That is the survivor's truth.

We in Village Laguna are the voice of everyman, everywoman. We refuse to be silent in the face of a bulldozing progress. We cherish what has gone before us. It is worth saving. When I sit over lunch at Jon Madison's Garden, I am surrounded by trees over a hundred years old. The sound of progress is stilled. A bare half-block away, I cannot hear the cars as they hurtle by. Trees muffle sound. Old trees muffle it best.

People sometimes dismiss Village Laguna as "too negative." They miss the point. They do not hear our voice. We stand for what is best in Laguna. There is nothing negative about an old building, an old syca-more, a creek that wends its way through a canyon. We insist on preserving that building, that tree, that creek. When they are threatened, we act.

We are movers and shakers, not watchers and waiters. We are doers. The sidelines are for other folk. It is not that we resist change. We resist change for the worse. We resist change that destroys. Listen again to Jon Brand thirty-four years ago: "Change is all about us, and the ability to absorb change is the ability to survive. But change can be controlled and channeled to keep Laguna a village. If the change is too drastic, the char-acter of this community will be radically transformed, and those values that attracted the artist, the man who marches to a different drum, the people who dislike suburbia, the family that wants a healthy environ-ment—these people will leave Laguna, and the village will be destroyed."

So we defy that destructive change. And we will be heard.

November 2005

When I was a kid in the Bronx, a penny went a long way. I could buy a string of Tootsie Rolls, stuck loosely together so I could snap them off and eat them one at a time—all six—for a penny.

Down in the subway, vending machines sold other chocolates for a penny apiece.

When I was a few years older and feeling like a big shot, I could buy a cigarette for a penny at the local candy store, where, of course, I could buy all sorts of penny candy.

A penny had value: "See a penny, pick it up; all the day you'll have good luck" had the ring of truth. I picked up many a penny lying in the gutter—and thought I had struck a bargain.

Today, have I got a bargain for you! You and I can buy back our town for half a cent. (Eat your heart out, Peter Minuit! No wonder the Dutch fired you when you blew a whole $24 to buy Manhattan!)

That's what the election on December 13 is about—a half-cent increase in our sales tax so we can pick up pennies, $10-million-plus of them, a half-cent at a time, over a period of six years. (Six years is the drop-dead time limit; the tax increase expires after six years.)

That money, translated into dollars as $10.2 million, will do more than pay salaries and repair roads, more than buy a new door for the fire station or pay the salary of a new marine protection officer to protect our fragile tide pools or repair the sagging Main Beach Park boardwalk. There's a pothole across from our house on Santa Cruz Street deep enough to tear a wheel off its axle. We'll be able to repair that pothole. And maybe the next time the Athens Group sees a piece of land it hasn't already trampled, we'll have a building inspector near enough by to say "Naughty, naughty." We'll protect our hills, gird our roads, clean up litter.

But, as I say, there's more to it than money. It's a vision thing.

When we walk on the Main Beach boardwalk, we'll be able to lift our eyes from what had once been a groaning board hinting at collapse. We'll look up instead at Seal Rock and the outline of Catalina Island. We'll look out at the horizon. We'll lift our eyes from our shoes and look at our shores. Money like that does buy happiness. It restores confidence. It instills a sense of safety. It makes Laguna even more livable.

No, we can't stave off disaster. Disaster just seems to like us. There always seems to be more black cloud than silver lining, so disaster will come. But we'll be ready, with money at work fixing our streets, money in reserve for any emergency. That's our vision.

I used to think six Tootsie Rolls for a cent constituted a great bargain. Now I've got a whole town ready to tax itself so we can all smile again. All we've got to do on December 13 is say yes, Yes, YES!

February 2006

Ah yet, ere I descend to the grave
May I a small house and large garden have.
— Abraham Cowley, *"The Wish,"* 1647

I have a small house—1,600 square feet, poky rooms
with nooks and crannies and books overflowing. The
garden, front and rear, is not particularly large, but it is
bountiful. Soon the locust tree, now starkly bare, will
leaf, and the jacaranda will begin to show blue on its
easternmost branch. The calla lilies are mostly vaga-
bonds, volunteers that have crept from front to rear. Two
so-called strawberry trees frame our walkway in front;
the eastern one gave us close to a thousand berries last
year. Bonnie is planting a basil pot for her pesto sauce.
We have one small rose bush and camellias, both white
and pink, and other stuff the names of which I sometimes forget: a princess bush, a cluster of gorgeous faux
heather, a rosemary plant I dust my thumb against and
drink in the odor. No grass that needs mowing; we are
old and lazy—blue fescue in front, mondo grass in back.

It is all small-scale. I come from New York City,
where thirty-three years have given me more than my
fill of bigness. Bonnie and I both worked in the Empire
State Building, but only on the fourteenth floor; ninety
more floors were overhead. Now, in Laguna, small is
what I cherish, what I am comfortable with. I see no
need for a house of 17,000 square feet and room for
twenty-two cars in a garage nearly three times larger
than our house. I see no need for mansions. "Need" is
the key word—"need," not "greed." Some people seem
to need Hummers. We drive a four-cylinder car, and
our next car, if there is to be a next car, will surely be a
hybrid or perhaps even a hydrogen-driven vehicle.

I have one crusade left in me. Let me win this one. I want to see an antimansionization ordinance that declares just how big "too big" is. It isn't a new thought. I have gathered information on twenty-seven cities, most of them in Marin County, where a friend of mine of fifty years sits on the Planning Commission in Larkspur and helped write the ordinance there that limits house size to a particular percentage of lot size. Aspen sets building size caps on lots of varying sizes, beginning with lots of 3,000 square feet (1,800-square-foot building cap) and ending with lots of 50,000 square feet or more (5,000-square-foot cap). Not only can this be done, but it is also being done, and it is not all that new. The Larkspur ordinance is twenty-four years old this year. I will take these numbers and the concept to my fellow Environmental Committee members, and we will decide what to do with them. What I wish for is a presentation to the City Council, and soon.

I would not tell anyone not to build a monster house—just don't build it here. Try Wyoming.

One more crusade before I bottom out, one last wish: no more monsters.

March 2006

A photograph on my desk shows a parachutist about to land where the ocean meets the wet sand. The parachutist was Roy Holm, mayor of Laguna Beach, leading a squad of skydivers who had leaped from a plane piloted by the astronaut Gordon Cooper. On hand were a thousand Lagunans celebrating the day, including vice mayor Carl Johnson and councilmembers Jon Brand, Charlton Boyd, and Phyllis Sweeney (all members of Village Laguna). The occasion was the official dedication of Main Beach Park, June 22, 1974.

Today, thirty-two years later, we ready ourselves for other feats that will require, if not life-threatening leaps into nothingness, at least dedication and hard work. We have to dig our heels into the sand and take our stand.

Do we want more mansions? Do we want the Montage to build its golf course in our wilderness park? Do we feel we must cave in every time a lawyer waves a lawsuit in our face? No, no, no.

Do we want to restore greatness to Laguna Beach? Yes.

It used to be easy. We invented a new vocabulary for Laguna, and just about everybody signed on. We in Village Laguna existed to save the village. We said, "Preserve the village atmosphere," and the people said yes. We said, "Keep the charm," and they said, "You bet!"

Unfortunately, those who would pave the village rather than save it hijacked the language. Suddenly everybody was an environmentalist, and everybody just loved that ol' village atmosphere.

Horsefeathers! They hijacked the words and forgot the music. They passed an antimansionization ordinance and forgot to give it teeth, so today we have a 17,000-square-foot house with a garage for twenty-two cars approved for a hilltop site. They pretend that it doesn't violate our mansionization ordinance. Well, if it doesn't, don't you think we need a better ordinance?

We want to build something else—a better Laguna. From the start, that's been Village Laguna's mission. Its first action was to defeat the construction of high-rises on our beaches and establish a citywide building-height limit. We are doers. The hijackers of language talk the talk; we walk the walk—nay, run the walk. We leap from planes if we have to.

We helped write the Downtown Specific Plan. We helped create the Greenbelt. Who was that stealth figure who crept about at midnight planting Burma Shave signs to stop the Irvine Company from blighting the canyon? That was Toni Iseman. Who picketed Donald Bren's house to keep more blight out? That was Lida Lenney. Both were Village Laguna members. Who marched in the canyon that day, thousands of us? The people of Laguna Beach, and we were in the vanguard. We've never quit marching and doing. We helped stop that first incursion of the golf course into the wilderness, and we're ready for the next. We fought oil drilling off the coast.

We shop Laguna—it's more than a slogan. We help the afflicted. We supported those affected by the 1993 wildfire. We supported those affected by the 1995 mudslides. We put on a show at the Forum Theater and sent the proceeds to the families of the firefighters and cops lost in the September 11 disaster. And we supported and will continue to support the victims of the Bluebird landslide.

We pitch in. We helped save the Art Museum. We helped keep the Festival and Pageant from being hijacked elsewhere. We are the first responders to hijacking. I could go on, but words won't do it. A council election is coming up. Ask the candidates how they feel about mansions and golf courses in the wilderness. Ask them how they will stand up to threatening lawsuits. Every time a city council throws up its hands and says to a lawyer "You win!" it makes it easier for the next lawsuit and the next.

Our job is to dig our heels in the sand, not bury our heads in it. Let's make sure we vote to save Laguna, not sell it. The time is now.

Walkers in Laurel Canyon, part of Laguna's Greenbelt.

July 2006

We've seen a flurry of letters to the editors of our local papers recently protesting the opposition to the proposed house on Mar Vista. This is fair enough, except for one element that appears in some of them: Their writers seem to think that the owner of the property can do anything he or she wants with it. This is nonsense. You think I can turn my house into a 24-hour bowling alley with rock music bursting out of every open window? You think I can build a house nine stories tall and block everyone's view? I can't, and you can't. The building code says no, and the zoning code says no. We must abide by the law.

Understand me—I'm not saying that the Mar Vista project violates any law. It does something else: It violates the concept of Laguna Beach. Rejection of this concept is also present in these letters. They contain a message to environmentalists, to preservationists, to those who believe in community rights, the idea that a house is part of a neighborhood and a neighborhood is part of a community. That's what we have here in Laguna Beach, a community—a sharing of values, a desire to live together in some sort of harmony with each other and with nature. I love this town. I love its streets. I love its houses. I love its people. It's not a perfect place, and I'm not sure I would want it perfect (what would I have to write about?). But I'm sure about one thing, and that's that I want to keep Laguna sort of like the Laguna I first saw a half century ago. The Mar Vista project, with its 17,000-square-foot house and 4,700-square-foot garage, isn't Laguna, and I protest.

Mar Vista is not alone. We have other disasters— huge houses overpowering neighborhoods. And when neighborhoods are destroyed, the community suffers.

We all suffer. In November we have a chance to save those neighborhoods. In November voters can decide that enough is enough—or, better, enough is too much. If there is a divide among the people who live here, it is that one group wants to keep this great little town just that way—a great little town—and the other seems to say that bigger is better, the developer's property rights rule, and anyone who thinks otherwise ought to shut his big mouth and crawl into his cave. Sorry, folks, that cave is my castle, and when I step outside, you'll know it.

April 2007

Nearly twenty years have passed since South Laguna left the uncertain existence as a ward of Orange County and entered, instead, the warm embrace of the city of Laguna Beach. North and South were united. South Laguna gained status as part of an enlightened incorporated city. Laguna Beach gained Ann Christoph. It was a clear victory for Laguna Beach.

It has not always been a smooth alliance. For some reason, South Laguna remains terra incognita—all those tiny streets, those narrow roadways, those signs warning off anybody who even thinks of parking in front of one of those much-too-small houses; hills not easily traversed, turnarounds that leave drivers sweaty and muttering imprecations. Well, we could understand all that, if we bothered. South Laguna loves cottages; South Laguna loves and cherishes its neighborhoods and will protect them against all intruders, foreign and domestic—particularly domestic. Yes, we are united, North and South, but it is not a love affair.

Take the matter of natural watercourses: A developer comes in and decides to build a residence or two or three on what clearly seems to be a natural watercourse. South Lagunans and others protest: "You can't build that close to a watercourse." And the developer retorts, "Yeah? Show me the watercourse on the city map." City staff says that the watercourse doesn't appear on the city's certified map. The Coastal Commission says that the watercourse is a stream and the project is appealable. Now the gloves come off. Who has priority here, the city or the Coastal Commission? Lawsuits are threatened. Time is wasted. Money is thrown away. Tempers fray.

It need not be. What has happened is a failure on the part of the city of Laguna Beach to do its job. At a City Council meeting on January 18, 1994—six-plus years after South Laguna had joined the city—the council unanimously passed a resolution that directed the city staff to place certain major watersheds and drainage courses in South Laguna on the city's maps as part of the General Plan. The watersheds and drainage courses are named. It is as clear a directive as can be imagined. The council of Kathleen Blackburn, Wayne Peterson, Lida Lenney, and Bob Gentry, under Mayor Ann Christoph, signed the resolution. And someone in City Hall chose to ignore the council's directive. City staff failed to pursue Coastal Commission certification of the map.

I do not know whom to blame—the city manager, the planning director, some unknown staffer—nor do I care. What matters is a quick fix. This is not a difficult task. It means reading and writing (so maybe it *is* difficult) and putting the seal of approval on something that should have been approved thirteen years ago. It means an end to the thus-far endless fights over whether there is or isn't a significant watercourse on a particular property a developer wants to build on. It means no more trips to the Coastal Commission to get a new opinion and throw more fuel on the fire. It means, once and for all, a fair deal for the residents of a beleaguered part of Laguna Beach.

This is more than a development issue put to rest: it is an acknowledgment of the existence of South Laguna. A resident of South Laguna can say, with some pride, "Look at us! We're on the map." And it again defines the roles of City Council and staff. The council makes policy; the staff carries it out. OK, staff, lift and carry. We're waiting, and we don't want to wait any longer.

May 2007

My second viewing of *An Inconvenient Truth* thrilled me even more than the first. Perhaps it was because of the identity of the sponsors of the showing in the Forum Theater. One sponsor was Village Laguna. Another was the Taxpayers' Association. The Republican Club signed on as a sponsor. So did the Democrats. Keep this up and soon we will no longer be a nation of blue states and red states. We'll be green states only.

The struggle goes on to save the planet. And save it we must. It will not be easy. It may, in fact, be the toughest problem humankind has ever faced. If Al Gore is right, and the science community seems to say he is, then we have already lost hunks of Greenland to ever-encroaching warmth. Chunks of Antarctica have fallen back into the sea. Polar bears are swimming fruitlessly in an ocean they once walked upon. But because most of the fault lies in us—we have caused this climate change—we need not look to the heavens for succor. The job is ours. We have created this murk of greenhouse gases. Let's change our habits. Walk, not drive. Some cities have already invoked a carless Thursday. We can close off our downtown to cars on Sundays. People will walk, bike, take the bus. No cars ever traverse the streets of Venice, Italy. Yet the city thrives. Tourists love it as it is.

We can learn to love Laguna with fewer cars. New York City is looking into putting a price tag on driving in midtown Manhattan. We are a nation of innovators. I don't know the answers to climate change. I just know that, together, we can get a handle on the problem and begin to turn it around. No, it won't happen soon. It took just a few days for Katrina to destroy much of New Orleans. We used to call such storms "acts of God." Now we know better. The acts are ours. We have to rewrite that drama. It will take time. Years, of course. Decades, surely. Generations will come and go, and slowly we will regain the lost ground. Slowly—oh, so painfully long and hard—the rising ocean must again fall, and ice again cover the Arctic.

Now let me turn back to Laguna, where we can more quickly grasp and twist that handle. We have lagged behind on so many environmental issues in Laguna, issues that while they go unanswered add to the woes of the planet. So let's take care of what we can, right here and now. Long journeys begin with small steps. We have cried out, long and loud and with others, for an antimansionization ordinance. No more monster houses! Monster houses are not green. They eat up our environment. We point to the success of building-size laws in Larkspur, Carmel, Santa Barbara, Aspen, dozens of other cities. But not ours. Why not? Well, the architects won't be happy. A monster house means a monster fee. And a client who wants his ego bolstered by having the biggest house on the block, he too will be unhappy when this city finally says, "This big and no bigger." That is the issue: community interest versus private interest. Which will prevail? I see no possible outcome other than the community winning. Community means all of us; private interest means somebody's wallet or somebody's foolish self-esteem. Is there really a contest?

The City Council must take the first step. Order the Planning Commission to craft an ordinance. Bring it to the floor of the city chambers and let the people hit the lectern—architects, builders, real estate brokers, and rich clients and, on the other side, just plain folks. Hear us, all of us, and pass the ordinance. It is the right thing to do. End monster houses, once and for all.

While I'm at it, what's happened to the Land Use Element and its newly revised draft? Why does it languish? It's been done and done and done. If it needs a final dusting, dust it, and bring it to the people.

This is how we will eventually go green, all over. It is not just replacing incandescent bulbs. It is not just a solar panel on your neighbor's roof or blue fescue in my garden. It is a community coming together. The Planning Commission answers to the City Council, and the City Council answers to us. We are the lords of this manor. We will green-up our manor.

The locust tree in my backyard has started to leaf. To me it is the beginning of a new year. Another spring. Let it be the last year before the City Council picks up the cry and joins with a single voice. Laguna will turn green. Tomorrow, the world. Well, if not tomorrow, sometime in a foreseeable future. Green states. Green nations. A green planet.

September 2007

You probably recall the death of a homeless person in Laguna Beach one summer night a few weeks ago, but let me refresh your memory: Gerald Hoy, 42, a Navy veteran, an alcoholic, and homeless, broke a window to enter the Laguna Resource Center in the canyon and in so doing gashed his hand. He crawled through the broken window, lay down on a sofa, and bled to death. Those are the facts. The why remains elusive. Again, permit me: Question: What was Gerald Hoy doing, breaking and entering the Center on so balmy a night? Couldn't he have slept in Heisler Park as he had so often before?

Answer: Yes, he could have, but he chose not to. He was a homeless man seeking, that night, a home.

That's as far as my intuition carries me. What does the homeless person lack that you and I have? A home—a place with four walls and a roof. I am helped here by the great poet Robert Frost, whose narrative poem "The Death of the Hired Man" is eerily similar to the fate of Gerald Hoy. In the poem, a nomadic worker comes back to a farm where he had worked before, ostensibly to help with the haying but really seeking a shelter and a place to die. The farm wife tells her husband, "He has come home to die," and when he questions "Home," she explains: "Home is the place where, when you have to go there, they have to take you in."

Gerald Hoy went to the only home he knew these days, the Laguna Resource Center. But on that night no one was inside; the door was locked. He assumed that he could enter. He must have felt that they had to take him in. He broke the window, cut his hand, and was found dead the next morning.

Up in Los Angeles, the *Los Angeles Times*'s dogged columnist Steve Lopez keeps digging into the problems of the homeless on his streets. He says of the city government that it deals with the symptoms of homelessness but not the root causes of the problem. I say, "Ditto here in Laguna." The symptoms are easily spotted (even if grossly exaggerated): drunkenness in public, urinating in the street, aggressive panhandling. But the causes? Many of the homeless are mentally disabled. Others are alcoholics, drug abusers. Some lost their jobs, their families, and their homes and took to the streets. Some are physically sick, beyond all of the above.

Gerald Hoy, I am told, probably did not have long to live, his liver was so shot by booze. I asked my friend Don Black, who is in charge of the Center on a volunteer basis, whether the homeless people he knows (and he knows every one by name) would accept a shelter rather than sleep in Heisler Park to be awakened by the toe of a cop's boot gently nudging them up and about. "Yes," he said. "They would."

So I begin from there. It won't solve the problem, but at least it supplies the missing link in their lives: home—a home you don't have to break into, a home you don't have to deserve, a home you can take for granted. Let's find one—buy it if it exists, build it if it doesn't, supply the shelter for our homeless. Too late for Gerald Hoy, but soon enough for others like him.

May 2008

At a recent Village Laguna board meeting held in the gorgeous hillside home of Barbara Dresel (and her husband Rick Holder), a member looked out across the valley at a huge swath of undeveloped land.

"What's with that property?" the member asked.

"It's R-1," Barbara answered.

Bonnie Hano corrected her. That hundred-plus-acre parcel is owned by the city as open space. Once it was R-1. We turned it around.

It didn't just happen, of course. This is the history: In the early 1970s, the owner of those acres proposed a hillside development that would include some 715 homes above Morningside Drive. It came before the Planning Commission; a commissioner told Bonnie and me about it, with the grave concern that the project would be passed that evening.

Back then, few Lagunans (other than the applicants) attended Planning Commission meetings. Bonnie and I and a neighbor, Bernie Luskin (who later became the first chancellor of Coastline Community College), were the only people in attendance. The three of us spoke against the project, citing safety concerns. Seven hundred new homes would mean close to 6,000 car trips a day in a box canyon with just one road in and out. We also argued that the neighborhood had not been noticed, and with some reluctance the commission agreed to continue the item to the next scheduled meeting date — by which time we had gone door to door and some 120 residents, all of whom were opposed to the gigantic development, showed up. It was turned down.

Nothing is ever turned down for good in Laguna, then or now. The theory of developers is "Wear 'em down." The owner came back with plans for 240 homes. Neighbors packed the room again. The commission turned down this version. Back they came again, this time for a mere 80 units. And back we came again, all those bodies. The commission voted it down again, unanimously. And the wearied owner said to the city, "Take the damned thing off my hands."

Which the city did, for $600,000, and zoned it open space.

So there it sits. Pristine. A lovely hillside untouched by the bulldozer's blade. A hundred-plus acres, owned by the people.

I hope the lesson is clear. The people count. When we show up in force, when we are united, we hold back the seemingly inevitable tide. This is Village Laguna's mission. We came together in 1971 and wrote an initiative to establish a citywide building height limit. Thirty-six feet, three stories, not an inch higher. That is how we defeated high-rise, here in Laguna, forever. No city in America had ever used the initiative process to establish a citywide height limit. We did it.

Once Standard Oil wanted to put up a gas station at the north end of town. A pine tree stood on the property. Standard said, "We'll have to chop it down." We said, "No you won't." Standard insisted that the tree was dying. We asked Fred Lang to look at it, as our arborist. He looked and declared the tree would last at least 20 years more. Which is longer than the name "Standard Oil" has lasted. The tree still stands.

This is what we stand for. This is what we speak for. We are the voice of old trees. We are the voice of unprotected hillside. Some people see it otherwise. We are, they say, too negative. We're always against something. They're the same people who think of property as a disposable commodity. We see it as our home. They are the ones who would demolish historic structures, chop down those trees, uproot the village legacy. And they think we're negative!

We brought a new and fresh vocabulary to Laguna, the words "village atmosphere" and "village character," the sense of human scale, the idea that bigger is not always better. We want to keep Laguna Laguna. It is our mission. We live by it. In a sense, we puzzle the other side. They think in terms of what's-in-it-for-me. They can't understand that there is nothing in it for us, except the life of this town we love.

January 2009

A few days before Bonnie and I arrived for the first time in Laguna Beach, on September 1, 1955, another family secretly fled Laguna in the depth of the night. They had been the objects of hatred, ridicule, vituperation, obscene midnight phone calls, and the like. They packed up their belongings and themselves, and they escaped. They were Jews.

Some time after Bonnie and I had settled into our new life here, we learned that certain men could not get their hair cut in our barbershops. They were black.

Later came a wave of young people into Laguna. They caroused, used drugs, drank, made music in the streets, and sat on curbs.

The Christmas 1970 "happening" in Laguna Canyon drew over 10,000 hippies.

They too were objects of derision and hate. An ordinance was passed by the City Council forbidding their sitting on the sidewalks and making music. A wiser Lagunan, Judge Richard Hamilton, trashed the ordinance as unconstitutional. A councilmember recommended dynamiting the caves in the Canyon so that these young people would be deprived of the caves for sleeping quarters each night. These were our hippies.

Women in Laguna were long denied access to power, always overlooked in appointments to boards, committees, and commissions. Seventeen appointments in a row were made, all to men. An officer of the Fair Political Practices Commission came to Laguna to put a stop to such discrimination.

Gays in Laguna led a closeted existence, afraid to come out and acknowledge their sexual orientation. A candidate for the City Council one year tried to ban gays from staining our sands at Main Beach with their presence.

All the above is a history of The Other. We're okay; you're not. It is a phenomenon not unlike discrimination elsewhere. I remember a good loyal Democrat here in Laguna who refused to vote for John F. Kennedy in 1960 because, she said, he would take his orders from the pope; he was a Catholic, and that was enough for her. For a while the city tried to stop the Hare Krishna kids from parading through our streets chanting their quiet songs. Foreign-born people trying to find hired work in Laguna became the targets of legal action. They were committing crimes, it was charged; they even fomented revolution—get rid of them.

Now it is the homeless. People object to being aggressively panhandled (though in my fifty-three years in Laguna I have never once been aggressively panhandled). They say that the homeless are dirty, foul-smelling, druggies, mental retards, and the like. Some of these things are true. The homeless are too often sick, too often shun others just as they are shunned by society. But mainly they are The Other.

It is time for this to stop. It is time for us to figure out how to bring the homeless back into the mainstream. It won't be easy. But it must be done. This is what we do here in Laguna.

We are a can-do community. The constituencies I listed above—Jews, blacks, women, gays—all have been accepted by the community. No, we aren't a unanimous loving family, but we are a family—contentious at times, squabbling at the dinner table, but communing together, breaking bread together.

I don't know how this will end. But I do know it has to start. One way to start is to take our anti-camping ordinance and get rid of the unconstitutional language that says people can't sleep on the beach at night. If you don't offer an alternative place to sleep, you can't stop people from sleeping on the beach or in the bushes. That said, we have to attack the causes of homelessness. We have to make sure the homeless have access to the Community Clinic and other medical and mental health facilities. I don't know what other steps should be taken. But I do know we must sit down together and work this out. It's clear that we have absorbed The Others in the past.

We have successfully confronted fire, flood, and slide. Now it's another form of disaster. Now it's the homeless. They are a relatively small group, though with job loss and foreclosures, they will probably increase in numbers. They have no voting power, though they are allowed to vote; I doubt that many do. It is up to us to take the steps to get this started. Village Laguna has not made the homeless a high-priority item. No matter. It is the item on my agenda that brings me close to tears when I meet with the street people and hear their stories. But I have also heard their music, their

songs, and their humor. Can we do something to nour-
ish these people, bring them into our own lives, absorb
them as we have absorbed others?

Yes, we can.

March 2009

Some forty years ago, give or take a decade, I read an article in a science magazine,"Why Do Rivers Meander?" Because it was written in science lingo, I did not get much out of it, but I think I learned that rivers are wild spirits, full of energy and with a wonderful wanderlust that takes them hither and yon. And in their wildness, they sculpt the crust of the earth, creating such wonders as the Grand Canyon. They are the earth's true architects. It is in their DNA; they do not like to be curbed, cribbed, confined. They especially do not like to be dammed. Damming a river is akin to violating its DNA. Do Not Abate.

Aliso Canyon and Aliso Creek

We are confronted with a river/creek problem in South Laguna. Aliso Creek is a polluted version of its original clean, wild self. Once it created Aliso Canyon, carving out its serene beauty. Today it is treated as something standing in the way of progress.

First, a brief history lesson. Aliso Creek is millennia old. The cities that surround it are still cutting their baby teeth. Think of them as the Terrible Twos. They throw tantrums. They also throw filth into the creek. They treat the creek as a trash bin.

Our problem is twofold. We have to clean the creek; we believe it should be done at its source. And we have to keep it from turning into yet another flood drain, its energy imprisoned between concrete walls. Clean the creek; keep the creek free. Any project that does not do these two things is a failed project.

We are facing a project called the SUPER Project, not because it is super or superior or anything other than an acronym. It is another piece of failure. When you cannot define your product, use an acronym. British Petroleum did not want American consumers to think that (1) it was foreign and (2) it was fossil fuel, so it became BP on your television screen with wind turbines turning merrily in the background. The SUPER Project hides its bones with flashy flesh. You might as well call it STUPOR Project: Senseless. Travesty. Useless. Poorly planned. Overpriced. Ridiculous—STUPOR. But word games won't solve problems. We have to take this project seriously. It has legs. Even Barbara Boxer has signed on.

To turn it into a feasible plan, we have to study it, come up with sensible alternatives, and sell the plan to the public. People are wary of what is going on. They don't trust the Army Corps of Engineers, a feckless agency that dams rivers and then un-dams them as the rivers die. And we are expected to laud the appointment of this agency to lead the proposed project. Common sense tells us that there must be a simpler, wiser, less costly plan than the one thus far presented.

So I advise you to study the project. This is just the beginning. But it's never too early to be heard. Speak up. We are the credible environmentalists in this town. We—you—are being called upon.

Now.

Seldom has an issue so erupted in angry rhetoric as has the issue of a marine reserve along the Laguna coast. Fishing would be prohibited in the reserve. The fishermen (and women and children) are screaming bloody murder. They see their livelihood threatened. They see their lifestyle destroyed. On the other hand are the environmentalists who want to see the Marine Life Protection Act validated here in Laguna.

The tussle is so polarizing that even God argues with God. At a meeting in the Aliso Creek Inn that brought together the two sides, a young fisherboy called out to me: "Read your Bible. Genesis 1:28." When I got home I read Genesis 1:28; it is God's declaration to Adam and Eve that they shall have dominion over all living things—the fish in the sea, the fowls in the air, the beasts that crawl upon the earth. But I read further and came across Genesis 6:19, God's edict to Noah to build an ark and stock the ark with two members of every species. I presumed God meant a male and a female. And Noah and his family and all the animal species went on to create a civilization anew.

I think we environmentalists win that one.

The fishing crowd points out that they have fished these grounds for years and some of them for generations. We who want to see a marine reserve established argue back: Yes, you have fished here for years and generations; all we want is a five-year respite, to replenish the depleted fishing store. Take a five-year break. Give up instant gratification. A two-pound lobster today will be a five-pound lobster five years hence. More money in your pocket and a better meal for chowhounds.

Lifestyle is argued. There is about the fishing institution an aesthetic character, a mystique. A Norman

Rockwell quality pervades the fishing scene. It is undeniably pretty.

A good friend of mine who is an inveterate and avid fisherman says that I should stand on a rock at Victoria Cove and watch a young fisherman cast his line into the dark sea. He says solemnly, "If you see that, you'll know what I mean." Yes, I know what he means. He sees something iconic, thrilling to the eye and spirit. It is an Ayn Rand moment.

Well, if recreational fishing were just this young poster boy, I would not object to permitting him to fish in the restricted area. But recreational fishing also includes a shipload of merry-making passengers coming down from Newport into our waters and drunkenly tossing their hooked lines willy nilly into an oceanful of children splashing about.

This is sport, the fishing gang cries. Kelly Boyd says he has been a sport fisherman for years and years. I have a different definition of sport. To me, sport is a contest between willing rivals, of equal or near-equal powers. The Bears and the Packers. The Giants and the Dodgers. Tiger Woods and the rest of the world. Federer and Roddick. If sport is to include a youngster spearing a Garibaldi lolling about in a bed of kelp, then I expect that the next new sport will be a bullfighter from Barcelona taking on a calf.

So the debate rages. We believe that the best reserve would be one that covers the entire Laguna coastline, from Abalone Point to below Three Arch Bay. With the new Edison reef, just below Three Arch, prepared to generate fifty tons of fish annually, there will be a plentiful harvest for fishermen.

But, they argue, how can you enforce such a stretch, seven miles long, three miles deep, with just one marine officer? Of course we'd like more officers, but a darkening economy makes that impossible. Still, we have dozens of ocean docents and a volley of volunteers ready to see that nobody fishes in that restricted area. We've seen too many tide pools robbed of their glorious population; we've seen the abalone die off. If there are any grunion still running, I haven't seen one in five years.

The question arises: Why are there fewer fish these days? One answer, of course, is pollution, and that is not the fault of fishermen. Our inland cities still treat Aliso Creek as a trash bin. This has to stop. Fishermen will tell you that the greatest loss of fish (other than from polluters) is from bigger fish eating smaller fish. And sea lions are hungrier still.

One young fisherman at the Aliso Creek Inn found it hard to believe that Laguna has a nonprofit that nurses sick or injured sea lions back to health and then gently dumps them back into the sea. "I would remove the 'endangered species' designation from sea lions," he says. Then he would remove the sea lions with his rifle.A volunteer from the sea mammal rescue group says that many of the beached sea lions are starving. There are so few fish.

I have not played the empathy card as yet. Too often we environmentalists are accused of being wimps, of being softhearted, of being a tad squishy. To which I plead guilty. But we are not alone. On magazine assignment years back I boarded a Polaris submarine in San Diego and spent forty-eight hours traveling beneath the sea up to Vallejo. During my stay, I spoke with the sonar technician, the man who shoots sonar rays into the sea to determine what lies before him. And when the ray hits something, it bounces back, enabling the sub to measure how far the object is from the sub. The sonar tech let me listen to the sound of the ray striking an object and the object responding. The sound was not unlike that of a maternity ward nursery. "What is that sound?" I asked the tech. "That's a school of shrimp," he said. "We've hit them. The shrimp are crying."

We are a community that protects life. Let's not lose this opportunity.

November 2009

On November 14, Bonnie and I will be honored as Villagers of the Year. A cynic says we are villagers without a village. I say, "Open your eyes."

That's village I see from the mullioned-pane window next to our computer—well, Bonnie's computer, which she permits me to use for this column. I remain a Luddite.

I do not own a cell phone. I still think Blackberry is what makes a jam. I do not know what a Facebook is. Nor do I want to know. I've lived eighty-seven years without knowing. Why confuse me further?

What do I see from my window? I see Randall Way. You never heard of Randall Way. I bet you never heard of Roosevelt Lane, either. It's in Laguna Canyon; you find it by a wooden street sign tacked to a tree.

Roosevelt Lane is six feet wide. City streets are 60 feet wide. How about Glomstad Lane? Osgood Court? Even the street we live on poses problems finding it. Santa Cruz Street is really two streets, one south of an arroyo and one north. One of them should be renamed. Don't let it be mine.

It's these cockamamie streets that make it a village. I love crooked streets. I love narrow streets. Yes, I know it's hell for Waste Management to turn around on Randall Way, but we cheer them on, and at Christmas time we tip the guys. They deserve it. Can you imagine tipping a garbage collector in New York? We're a village.

Of course, it's changed since we arrived back in 1955. The town has swallowed South Laguna and Bluebird Canyon and Arch Beach Heights. None of those areas was in the city of Laguna when we arrived. The 6,000 people have become 24,000. Once a truck toiled up

Temple Hills twice a week to sell water to the handful of houses on Top of the World. Today the jam-packed neighborhood has its own water (for much more money). We used to have no smog. Then we began to import it from Los Angeles. Now we create our own.

Mary Zava, who lived on Jefferson Way, near the top of Bluebird Canyon, rode her horse Glissanda all over Bluebird Canyon. Mary and Bob Zava, an architect and artist, were our closest neighbors. Actually, Glissanda was closer, in a corral, where our two-year-old daughter, Laurel, would sometimes crawl to eat the wild mushrooms that grew in Glissanda's manure. I kid you not.

Another Bluebird neighbor was a dentist who rode his skateboard to his office on Glenneyre every day. His reception room had no chairs. But it did have a gorgeous receptionist who sat cross-legged on the floor and served tea to waiting patients, all of whom also sat on the floor and chanted "Om." One day the dentist and his receptionist closed down the office and moved to a commune up north. I guess our village was becoming too stodgy for them.

But it remains a village. It looks like a village. It smells like a village except when the sewer pipes break. It sounds like a village. The sound of a city is clatter. The sound of a village is birdsong.

We have houses on the 500 block of Oak Street that you can't see from the street. Each house has a bridge that crosses over a sometimes dry creek. That's how you get to the front door. Tell me that's not a village.

So we're being honored. We've worked hard to keep Laguna Laguna. So have a zillion others. This is a town that has survived crises. Fire. Flood. Landslide. I guess it can survive us. Meanwhile, we keep doing what we do most of these days, going to our doctors in

Newport Beach, whose reception rooms have chairs and whose patients aren't chanting "Om." But then nobody ever accused Newport Beach of being a village.

Arnold and Bonnie Hano: Villagers of the Year 2009

April 2010

If you would like a glimpse of what Laguna Beach will look like a few years hence, here's a preview, based on the actions of the City Council at its April 6 meeting. No more plastic bags at the checkout counter. If you want a paper bag you may have to pay for it. So why sweat it? On our own we can simply say no more plastic, no more paper at all. We will shop the way our cousins who live in Aix-en-Provence shop every day. They carry permanent bags with them, smartly knitted bags that last for years. Bonnie and I would tag along to the bakery, the butcher shop, the fruit stands, the long tables of fragrant cheeses. Shopping this way was the second-best thing we did in France—eating always the first best. The French eat well, drink well, and still manage to outlive us.

Now city staff in Laguna will look into how best to get such shopping bags into each household. It will happen. And plastic bags will no longer choke marine life. And fewer paper bags mean fewer trees to be toppled.

It's been suggested that the house where Hortense Miller lived be nominated for a spot on the National Registry of Historic Places. Assuming that all goes well, the house will have a plaque on the outside wall attesting to the fame of Hortense Miller's home.

Hortense would have scoffed at such ostentation, but Laguna will be the better for it. Houses are worth saving. Gardens are worth saving.

Hortense Miller deserves attention. The world has become too citied. Here, on the lip of Allview Terrace, we leave the city behind and glory in the wonder of nature.

The Hortense Miller home and garden

We still have no effective antimansionization ordinance, but a mind-set seems to be developing—that mansions and neighborhood compatibility can't coexist. Not everyone agrees. The owner of a house on Driftwood Drive decided to add a second story plus some decks and a larger garage, more than doubling the size of the original residence—all this in a neighborhood of mostly modest-sized one-story houses. When the project reached the Design Review Board, neighbors opposed it. DRB okayed the plan. Two neighbors appealed to the City Council. Loss of light, air, and privacy became the issues, all of which could be remedied if excess mass were whittled down. The council agreed with the appellants and sent the project back to DRB for modification. DRB made minor changes. The neighbors appealed a second time, and the council agreed with them a second time. Neither the Planning Commission nor the DRB appreciates the council's occasional overturning of its decisions, but the council remains the final arbiter.

I don't know how it will play out. But I do know that individuals can stand up to mansions, and sometimes it is the mansion that yields.

You will see fewer spear guns on the beach. You will see fewer dead fish washed up on the sand or belly up in the water after hook-and-release. You will see more and lusher kelp beds. The Marine Mammal Center will see fewer half-starved sea lions, unable to find their usual catch of fish. The council reiterated its support of a marine reserve the entire length of the city's shoreline. No spears. No hooks. No traps. For five years, if the Department of Fish and Game agrees, there will be a respite, a time-out for fishing in our immediate waters. The lobsters will fatten up. The fish stock will grow. Kelp beds will be replenished. Our ocean will thrive.

Such was the will of the City Council on April 6. The official color was green. The official dessert was Village Flavor.

July 2010

When I was a kid in the Bronx, my brother and I would go up to the roof after supper and stare at the starry sky. Alfie, three and a half years older and decades wiser, would point out the Big Dipper, and we would trace a path from the bottom of the cup to Polaris, the North Star. He would point to a faint red smudge and say, "That's Mars. God of War."

I would nod gravely. And we would find Orion as he strode the top of the sky with his dog at his heel.

Later, during World War II, after the battle of Attu, the most remote part of America, near the Arctic Circle, I would sit outside my tent while the sun slowly set, and I would watch the stars come out. They thronged the sky. Isaac Asimov in one of his sci-fi novels said you could see 4,000 stars with the naked eye. Some years later in another novel, he upped the figure to 6,000. I had no way of counting the stars at Attu, but I would not be surprised if I had been looking at 60,000. One night I counted six falling stars as they tumbled one at a time through the heavens and smashed into dozens of white flames when they hit the atmosphere.

I have not seen a falling star in years. I cannot remember when I last saw the Big Dipper. Orion has vanished. We have lost our stars. Mars hides behind a shield of haze. A solid curtain blocks off the Milky Way. I would guess that there are children today who have never seen a falling star.

For years Toni Iseman has been striving to bring back the stars. Long a foe of noise and neon, she has made our days better, and now she wants to give us back our nights. On her suggestion, the City Council has directed the Planning Commission and the Environmental Committee to work on an ordinance regulating lighting, and in the next few months they will be reporting on their progress.

We misuse our city lights. We point them down and we point them up. Down is good; it makes our streets safer. Up is stupid. It throws a haze over our city. With smart street lighting, we can see a speeding car, we can see an intruder, and we can also see Orion once more, astride the universe, his belt aglitter with diamonds and his faithful dog at his side.

March 2011

The events that have racked Wisconsin remind me of events that led to the birth of Village Laguna. Instead of a union-busting governor we had a City Council consumed by paranoia over hippies and dogs. One councilmember, Ed Lorr, believed that if he could get rid of dogs, their hippie owners would flee to more friendly environs. The council passed an emergency ordinance banning dogs from all parks and beaches. Unfortunately, it forgot that Laguna is a dog town. We dog owners put on a display of force—we paraded our dogs, and we carried signs.

We discovered that the way to fight an ordinance was through a referendum. We filed notice of referendum, gathered petitions with the names of registered voters, and placed our petitions on the desks of the council. Eventually we agreed on a compromise—half the parks would be verboten for dogs, and the beaches would allow them during early morning and evening hours. Nobody liked the compromise, which is a definition of a perfect compromise.

Perhaps emboldened by a sort of victory, the council then made its next mistake. It looked at a recent hotel, the Surf and Sand, and decided it liked what it saw—a building constructed in a zone that limited such structures to 35 feet in height but then added 23 more feet via the variance process. It now wanted a new zone in Laguna, a mile-plus of high-rise buildings from Broadway to Bluebird Canyon Drive—100 feet tall, ten stories high, plus whatever the lax variance law would allow.

Many of us who had been involved in fighting for dogs got together and formed a small committee to take on this new zone. A landscape architect, Roger McErlane, built a model of what our beachfront would look like from Broadway south. We brought the model, covered with a sheet, to the Planning Commission hearing on the new zone. When the item came up, we whisked off the sheet, and there was the model of tomorrow. A commissioner said after the meeting, "When we saw the model, we knew it was all over. We could never have that zone."

This time we took the initiative route. We wrote an amendment to the city's building code prohibiting building heights in the future from going over three stories, 36 feet. And we started to have petitions signed. The first weekend we had 1,016 names. After a month we had 4,000 names. Not everybody in town agreed with us. The City Council did not, nor did the Planning Commission, the Chamber of Commerce, the Board of Realtors, or the *Laguna News-Post*. On our side we had the Citizens' Town Planning Association. No other organization, just the people. The council could have accepted our petitions and dropped the zone. It chose instead to fight. Our committee called itself the Yes on August 3 Committee for the date of the election. On that day we carried every precinct and won by over three to one citywide.

The next day's *Los Angeles Times* put it on the first page. We had become the first city in America to use the initiative process to establish a citywide building height limit. I believe we remain the only one.

And on that next day the Yes on August 3 Committee became Village Laguna, so named by lawyer Ralph Benson.

Wisconsin could learn from our history. We now have forty years behind us, and the fight continues. There's open space to be preserved, small-town quality to be kept, heritage houses and old trees to be saved—or

lost. There are homeless to be housed—or driven off.
There's greatness to be achieved—or squandered.
So cheer up, Wisconsin. You still can win.
The people, yes.

Lagunans march in protest of a ban on dogs on the beach.

April 2011

Ralph Benson dropped by the other week, and he and Bonnie and I had lunch at Sapphire. Ralph is the director of the Sonoma Land Trust. He gathers up parcels of land and turns them into open space in perpetuity. He is the Derek Ostensen of Sonoma. Forty years ago, as a young lawyer in the County Counsel's office, he joined our campaign to halt a new zone that would have permitted high-rise hotels on our shore. He knew, however, that by law we couldn't use the initiative to amend zoning. "How about amending the building code?" we suggested. He brightened at that, read the building code, and came up with a section that dealt with mass and scale. "Amend that," he said, "and you'll be in business." And so we proceeded.

We met every Tuesday evening in the back of David Rosen's art studio on Coast Highway. The front door was always open. We wrote letters. We had legal advice: Ralph Benson, Bill Wilcoxen. We had a water engineer. We had a landscape architect. We collected names on our initiative petitions the old-fashioned way. Our volunteers sat at tables outside the grocery stores and in front of the library and in the breezeway next to the post office. Others took clipboards up into the hills. We signed up Lagunans by the barrel.

One thing we had decided early: we would not run a campaign that asked for a No vote. We knew that if we defeated a high-rise zone, one would pop up elsewhere, so we agreed that our initiative would establish a city-wide building height limit. How high? We tried 38 feet, and Pete Ostrander, an architect on the City Council, nodded that he could live with it. Ralph Benson then suggested that we lower it to 36 feet; a multiple of 12 feet seemed sellable.

The other side did what it could. The *News-Post* decided that we were receiving all our money (what money?) from out of town. It had two planning commissioners write columns explaining how terrible our initiative would be. About a week before the election, Vern Taschner got a judge to declare the initiative illegal. Bill Wilcoxen put on his seven-league boots and whipped down to San Diego to an appellate court to ask what was illegal about it. Let the election come, he argued, and if we won, then the court could decide whether what we had done was legal. The court agreed, and on August 3 the election was held.

When the polls closed I drove to the nearest polling station and watched them count 10 ballots. This precinct came in 7 to 3 for us. I drove off to another precinct and listened to another 10 votes being counted. This one was 9 to 1. I whisked off to a third. This one was closer, 6 to 4. Total: 22 Yes, 8 No. I went home, mixed myself a very dry Martini, and toasted myself, the city, and good sense.

We had three hundred people to our house for the party. We had won 3,700 to 1,200. Everybody who had been involved was there. The *News-Post* sent its main reporter, Chuck Ramsay, over. When he came in, Frank Maxwell—who used to appear on TV crime shows as a judge or a cop and was a very nice man but strong as an ox—picked him up and shook him over the lip of our deck, forty feet above the ground. Ramsay yelped, "But I brought a six-pack!" Frank put him down and dusted him off, and we drank until two in the morning.

At the next City Council meeting, Roy Holm had our initiative voted on by the council, and it passed unanimously. When I attended my next meeting of the Design Review Board, our chair, Chris Abel, said, "Congratulations! Damn you!"

So, how about a citywide celebration of forty low-rise years? Let's party!

August 2011

The day after our initiative victory in 1971, the Yes on August 3 Committee dissolved itself and immediately regrouped as Village Laguna. The name came from Ralph Benson. I was chosen to serve as its first president. We began to meet in members' homes. We had members but no membership cards. We paid no membership dues. We had no bylaws. When we sought to take some action we seldom counted noses. We used a system similar to the Quaker "sense of the meeting." Very close votes—10 to 9, 18 to 16—tended to split the group. We sought consensus. It would be years before we would incorporate ourselves.

Celebrating the success of the high-rise initiative forty years later. From left to right: Eric Jessen, Bonnie Hano, Roger McErlane, Phyllis Sweeney, and Arnold Hano.

When I look back, I think the old days were better. We had a sense of empowerment. When we used the words "village atmosphere," the other side trembled. We won elections. Phyllis Sweeney became a council-member and the first woman mayor of Laguna Beach. Yes, Helen Keeley had won a seat before Phyllis, but I guess the four guys on the council could not go the next step and ever vote her mayor. Phyllis became mayor and started a marvelous line of women mayors, many from Village Laguna: Sally Bellerue, Bobbie Minkin, Lida Lenney, Ann Christoph, Toni Iseman.

Eventually, of course, the pendulum swung back. Every candidate for the council learned to say "village atmosphere." They all became "environmentalists." Of course, they caved in when faced with yet another mansion.

So it goes. That is the nature of a pendulum. And no matter, they can't erase the forty years of low-rise.

Perhaps the number forty isn't as catchy as twenty-five might have been, or fifty or a hundred. It's such a routine number. Yet, it's forty, a number both sacred and profane. God's wrath dropped rain for forty days and nights to launch Noah on his way to a better world, he and his family and his cargo of every animal species. Moses talks about the Jews' wandering for forty years in a wilderness. Jews fasted for forty days and nights. On the other side, Lizzie Borden killed a parent with forty whacks and then the remaining parent with forty whacks plus one. And forty is also mundane. Walter Pitkin glorified middle age with his book *Life Begins at Forty.*

I can't conceive of a future beyond, let's say, next Thursday. Fifty years will be well beyond my reach. So I think it's a good thing that it's forty years. We'll toast forty and hope that another forty will follow and our village will remain a village, Laguna will remain Laguna.

We will come together on September 12 at a dinner at Tivoli Terrace in a spirit of fellowship. We should pledge to honor not just the words "village atmosphere" but the concept. We must honor human scale. Big is not necessarily better.

We will bring together again that band of brothers who back in 1971 stood up to power and, in fact, wrested it away from those who thought they were invincible.

The poet Ralph Hodgson wrote: "Time, you old Gypsy Man, will you not stay?" And the answer is clear: No, Time will not stay. Time will not stop. Time is inexorable. But memory will stay. Memory will stop. Memory will remain until it becomes history. We honor that memory and the makers of that history.

What we all did was to make sure we can always see our ocean. It must never be otherwise. That is our honor. This is our pledge.

January 2012

George Bernard Shaw once wrote, and I murmur my
amen, "The reasonable man adapts himself to the world.
The unreasonable one persists in trying to adapt the
world to himself. Therefore all progress depends upon
the unreasonable man."

Or woman.

When I finished speaking to a Laguna Beach Historical Society meeting a few weeks ago, I was asked
who had been my heroes. I flubbed the question. I
muttered something incoherent and went home, and
the next day I thought of an answer. First, I thought of
the unreasonable Jim Dilley and the slightly more reasonable Bob Gentry. Each man created extraordinary
change. Dilley persuaded wealthy landowners to give
him land. Pretty soon we had our Greenbelt. Unbeliev-
able. Gentry became the first avowedly gay mayor in
California. He opened closets for gays and our minds
to fair play. I don't know how each man did it. Presto!
They changed our world. Yet I somehow don't think of
either man as my hero. Silently, almost unaware I found
myself thinking of another person. Mary Gray.

Who, you may ask, was Mary Gray? An unreasonable person, a marvelous person, a mover of the world
in quiet ways. Mary Gray spanned virtually our past
century. Born in 1901, she died in 1991, a day short of
her ninetieth birthday. She and her husband, Fitzhugh
Gray, owned the house just south of Treasure Island,
having purchased a coastal lot with 250 feet of ocean
front for a paltry $6,000 shortly after Pearl Harbor Day.
The fear of Japanese submarines shelling California
shores sharply drove down the cost of such lots. Mary
worked part-time as a social worker; her clients were

senior citizens, most of whom were years younger than she.

So far nothing particularly unreasonable.

Mary and Fitzhugh entertained; they built fire pits on the sand below, and we all ate burgers and hot dogs. And we drank martinis. This was county, not city, so an occasional deputy sheriff would wander by and cluck at us for having alcohol on the beach. So we'd invite him to join us. Which he did. Son Edward would strip abalone shells from barnacled rocks and Mary would pound the meat tender, and we ate abalone steaks twenty minutes old. Still, nothing unreasonable. Nothing heroic.

But something else was going on in that house that I knew nothing of. Bonnie knew, but women confide in women; men are left guessing. This is what distinguished Mary from others. Pregnant young women would go down to Mexico for their back-room butcher shop abortions. Abortion was illegal in the States. So girls, some as young as sixteen, would be driven across the border, undergo their procedures, and then be told to leave. The no-longer pregnant girls, bruised and perhaps still bleeding, would be driven some eighty miles to the Gray house. Mary would take in these wounded children. Give them a clean bed. Tend to them. Feed them. Nurse them back to health. Replace guilt and shame with a sense of worth. Somebody had cared. When they were able to do so, they would leave, for home or wherever.

Like the houses that harbored runaway slaves during the Civil War, this house on Coast Highway was a station on an underground railway. Here Mary Gray changed the lives of these wounded young. She set them free of the bondage of victimhood. She gave them a better world. An unreasonable woman, Mary Gray. My hero.

From left to right: Laurel Hano, Bonnie and Arnold Hano, Mary Gray and her daughter Lizzie

February 2012

This month marks my ninetieth birthday. The fact astonishes me, overwhelms me. I remember Lindy's solo flight. Dempsey's Long Count. Babe Ruth's home runs. Clara Bow. One day, sitting in the Polo Grounds bleachers, I heard a plane, screamingly close, blaze by. It was young Howard Hughes setting a transcontinental speed record, west to east. I was born in Warren Harding's tenure. World War I—it wasn't called that; it was the Great War— had ended, but as of my birthdate, March 2, 1922, American troops were still fighting Russia's Red Army.

Wars have marked my life. I hate war. I hate its insanity. If I have one lofty goal remaining, I want to see a Peace Academy established in the United States. We're up to our ears in war academies —Army, Navy, Air Force, Merchant Marine, Coast Guard, academies where our youth go to learn how to make war better. We have no equivalent Peace Academy, where young men and women would receive a college education and major in peace. My curriculum in four words: Why war, how peace? Put George Mitchell in charge. Send its graduates to the hot spots in the world, where they would bring their know-how to our consulates and embassies, to our UN delegation, congressional offices, State and Defense briefings. Why not?

I have two major regrets in life. One is that I didn't get off my keister and join the marchers at that bridge in Selma. I wanted to go, but I didn't. The other, far more deep-seated, is that my brother was killed in World War II. He was simply the best big brother any kid ever had. He always knew what was going on. He would say, "Let's go down to 46th Street. They're selling something called pizza pie." He taught me to read when I was three. He told me about girls. When Pearl Harbor pulled us into the war, we did not wait to be drafted. We each volunteered. He ended up in the Air Force, as a bombardier on a B-17; I found myself in the 7th Infantry Division. In combat we were some 9,000 miles apart, in different combat zones. We wrote to each other regularly. My last letter to him came back unopened and stamped "MIA," Missing in Action. His plane had been shot down. Later they found his body. At war's end I came home only slightly the worse for wear; he came home in a box. He remains my big brother, my older brother, though he died at age twenty-five back in 1944. The flag that draped his casket is in an attic in our house. I used to go up and hug that flag; I don't any longer. "Let it go," I whisper to myself, but I never do. That was the worst moment of my life, his death.

Bottom right: Arnold's brother, Alfred Hano, Lt., Bombardier

The best moment had come some years earlier, during the Great Depression. My father, whom I sometimes describe as the only downwardly mobile Jew I ever met, had been a lawyer whose practice dried up after the Great War. He landed a job as a paper salesman for his Uncle Phil. Then Uncle Phil died, and Pop was fired by Phil's two sons. Pop came home early in 1934 with his commission in his hand. Seventy-eight cents.

My mother said scornfully, "You should have thrown it in their faces." He hadn't. Seventy-eight cents in 1934 would have bought 13 quarts of milk.

Pop went looking for work. Every day, seven days a week, he would place a sheet of newspaper (a whole edition of the *Times* cost 2 cents) on a chair in the kitchen and black his shoes. Then he would go out into that jungle of joblessness and look for work. We'd moved from an apartment in a six-story house with an elevator for which we paid $75 a month to a three-story walkup for $35 a month. He went out every day for six months. Then one evening, just before supper, we heard his steps on the stairs, lighter, quicker. The door burst open. He had a job! We all shrieked. He took off his suit jacket and held out his arms to Mom. "Milady," he said, and "Master," she replied, and they began to waltz around the kitchen table. My brother held out his arms and I grabbed him and we followed, screaming, laughing, careening wildly about that white enamel table in the single most joyous moment of my life.

So it went. Depression and war and marriage and kids and death. And I live on. I wonder why. I wonder how. I keep thinking that each column will be my last. But then I ask my wonderful editor, "What next?" and we try to decide what's next.

Next is life. Next is continuing. Next is gently putting aside regret. Next is placing my hand on my wife's sweet back each night.

Arnold Hano Biography

Arnold Hano was born in New York in 1922. His first job was as a copy boy at the *New York Daily News,* and after serving in the Army in the Pacific during World War II he became managing editor at Bantam Books and then editor-in-chief of Lion Books.

In the early 1950s he and his wife, Bonnie, looking for a better place to raise their daughter, happened upon Laguna Beach and were immediately struck by the beauty of the place and the congeniality of its residents. They settled there in 1955 and quickly became involved in local issues. Bonnie helped establish the Free Clinic, and Arnold discovered that a black man couldn't get a haircut in Laguna and helped to change that. When in 1971 the City Council ordered the Planning Commission to establish a new zone to permit high-rise hotels along the oceanfront, Hano and others responded with an initiative passed by the public that limited building heights to thirty-six feet citywide.

Arnold taught writing at the University of Southern California, Pitzer College, and the University of California, Irvine. In addition to the 200-plus columns from which this collection was chosen, he wrote hundreds of magazine articles and twenty-six books, perhaps the best-known of which is a classic account of the first game of the 1954 World Series, *A Day in the Bleachers.* Until recently he wrote a monthly column for the newsletter of Village Laguna, an environmental organization he helped found. Village Laguna's mission is to preserve and enhance the unique village character of Laguna Beach, where the Hanos still live.

Made in the USA
San Bernardino, CA
14 March 2018